What the experts have said . . .

Here is a sample of the reviews that different editions of this book have received . . .

"This is one of those little gems that in years to come will be accepted as a standard strategy for home loan borrowers . . . shows how you can cut the term of your home loan significantly."
• **Personal Investment Magazine**

"Save a bundle on your home loan."
• **The Sunday Times**

". . . this book is an excellent summary and detailed analysis of methods by which mortgages can be effectively eliminated."
• **WA Business News**

". . . gives us hope that we can achieve freedom from our mortgage before a ripe old age."
• **Your Mortgage Magazine**

"It's like having your money do aerobics."
• **Mortgage Know How Magazine**

"Strategies for saving a bundle on home loans."
• **The Melbourne Age**

"This book shows you step-by-step how you can own your home years sooner."
• **Perth Woman Magazine**

"Save thousands on your home loan."
• **The Australian Women's Weekly**

"This book is an invaluable resource for any home owner wanting to save thousands of dollars in interest payments and own their home years sooner. I thoroughly recommend it."
• **Suresh Rajan - Financial Commentator**

D0063933

What readers are saying . . .

"...since April of this year, we have done the following (by using the Mortgage Elimination™ System as described in this book): paid off our $5,000 credit card, paid off our $5,000 personal loan, and saved $8,000... Meanwhile, our mortgage (which was $130,000 when we started) will be over and done with in four and a half years. I have now passed your website address (no one is getting my book!) on to lots of people, and I am getting the same stories from them. Thanks to you, our lives have changed completely. My stress levels are much lower, our marriage is better, and we have our priorities straight. Thanks again Mr. Gill."

• Darralyn Duffy

"It was going to take me 18 years to pay off my home loan the traditional way. I'm now going to pay it off in 4 years 9 months and save $90,000 in interest by using this system."

• Lou Athanasiu

"My original loan term was 26 years. I'm now forecast to pay it off in under 15 years using this system."

• Patrick Clark

"It was going to take me 12 years to pay off my home loan. Thanks to this book, I'm now going to pay it off in 6 years and save $30,000 in interest."

• Teresa Schofield

"We paid off our 20 year mortgage in 4 years and saved $97,000 in interest by using the information in this book."

• Nick and Christine Randall

"I'm 26 years old, and I should own my first home by the time I'm 32."

• Emma Mann

"Just like to congratulate you on your book. We have changed to the type of loan you recommended and have only been set up for a couple of months. We are further ahead now than what we were in a couple of years with our old loan. I have recommended your book to many people."

• Steven & Karena Ross

"The thing I do know, is that I wish I'd discovered it (this book) 20 years ago."

• Jeff Newman

How to
OWN YOUR HOME
Years Sooner!
without making
extra ∧ payments
interest

by Harj Gill

www.MortgageFreeUSA.com

American Mortgage Eliminators™ Publishing
YELM, WASHINGTON

First Published in Australia January, 1997
First USA Edition November, 2003
2nd Edition April, 2004

ISBN   0-9742676-0-0
LCCN   2003094936

BULK ORDERS: This book is available at quantity discounts. For further information, please contact the publisher via e-mail - Orders@MortgageFreeUSA.com

This book is designed to provide information in regard to the subject matter covered. The purpose of this book is to educate. The author, editors, and publisher shall have neither liability nor responsibility to any person or entity with respect to any perceived loss or damage caused, directly or indirectly, by the information contained in this book. It is recommended that you seek independent financial advice before proceeding with any action.

Contents

Acknowledgments

I would like to begin by acknowledging all my readers over the years that have applied my Mortgage Elimination™ System and provided invaluable feedback. You are the inspiration and foundation of this book. This includes all of you who have sent me comments about the difference my books have made in your lives - thank you for opening your hearts to me.

To my mother, thank you for giving me this wonderful gift called Life. I will never forget when you worked all those years as a factory hand on night shifts to make ends meet. With all my heart, I am grateful for your love, sacrifice, and continuing kindness.

To my lovely Lisa, you fill me with joy everyday. I absolutely love your passion for life and sharing it with me.

To Perry and Krystina, thank you for your constant support and wise counsel.

To Lisa, Justin, Scott, John, Sherry, Jeevan, and Cate, thank you for being a 'dream-team' because it is an absolute pleasure to work with you as my associates.

To the glory of GOD - the giver of this most precious of all gifts, called Life.

There are so many more people that I have had the privilege of knowing in my Life so far, and there will be many more. So at the risk of leaving you out, I will simply say, thank you ALL for making me a better person.

And finally to you, my new readers, thank you for allowing me to share in your journey of Owning Your Home Years Sooner.

Sincerely,

Harj Gill
CEO - American Mortgage Eliminators™, LLC

Read Me First

*"Life is a series of choices, and
it's up to us to make wise choices."*

- Morrel Perry -

I want you to take a moment and imagine what it would be like to completely Own Your Home. Maybe you could retire earlier and go on more vacations, or upgrade the car. Perhaps having a holiday house near the beach, or in the country is what would really make you happy.

Well, whatever your desires, it sure would be nice to have the financial freedom to exercise those choices, wouldn't it?

In most cases, these seem like far away dreams for most people; however, just about all of my readers are having to take them seriously because their dreams of being financially free are now well within their grasp.

In this book, I will introduce you to some of these everyday people who have saved tens of thousands of dollars in interest by applying the simple Mortgage Elimination™ System I will share with you.

> **Mortgage Elimination™ System**
> My unique program that helps you take charge of your home loan and pay it off years sooner.

All of these people, some of whom you will meet in this book are not famous or overly wealthy. They are just ordinary people who no longer wanted to be enslaved by a 30 year mortgage and made the decision to apply my system to break free.

For example:

Martin & Genevieve, a young working couple who reduced their $100,000 home loan from 25 years to 5 years and saved over $56,000 in interest.

Bill and Greta who had a 25 year home loan and were able to reduce it to 12 years 7 months and will save $93,773 in interest.

David & Sheryl, a single income couple who reduced their $101,313 home loan from over 20 years to 9 years 11 months and will save $83,216 in interest.

As I have come to expect, the initial reaction of every one of these people when they found out just how quickly they could pay off their home or investment loans was, *"I don't believe it!"*

However, after only the first month of following my unique Mortgage Elimination™ System, they were achieving their forecasted results and were well on their way to Owning Their Homes Years Sooner.

While reading this book, you will be able to follow simple, step-by-step explanations of what these people did to dramatically reduce the term of their home loans.

Celebrating the journey to get here

I know from first hand experience that one of the potential repercussions in this country, as a result of this book, will be a swath of people getting angry and upset that their lender didn't tell them about this system years ago. Furthermore, you will see a lot of these people airing their grievances in the media.

To counteract this reaction in Australia, some of the biggest banks in that country tried to discredit me and this system when my original book was launched there in 1997. Fortunately for me, I always believe that you can only fool all of the people some of the time, and my books on mortgage elimination became instant best sellers with over 150,000 copies sold. This was mostly done through direct mail order due to word-of-mouth recommendations from excited readers who wanted their friends and family to save money on their home loans too!

Over the years, these books have received so many rave reviews from respected financial publications and commentators in Australia that the Mortgage Elimination™ System I am about to share with you has now become a part of the national psyche. So much so that in the early part of 2003, the Australian subsidiary of HSBC bank (one of the world's largest banks), developed a home loan product in accordance with the recommendations in my book and started giving away a copy of it to anyone who inquired about their new home loan (see Appendix 1). If you know anything about the banking industry, you will appreciate that my book and system had to undergo nearly five months of assessment through this bank's legal department before they approved the campaign on behalf of the bank. I just wanted to share this information with you, in case you are skeptical about this revolutionary Mortgage Elimination™ System.

Getting down to business

If you were to meet me personally, you would find that I am an eternal optimist at heart and believe that there are always two ways to look at any given situation in life. In this instance, we can either choose to be victimized by what was the status quo, or we can choose to empower ourselves with new knowledge and *make wiser choices.*

I agree that there are a lot of things the banks can improve upon in delivering their services, but let's put everything into perspective with these three facts that you must keep in mind:

FACT 1: Your bank or lender is a business, and like any business, one of their main objectives, and right, is to make a profit.

FACT 2: Your lender is not a charity organization and therefore is NOT obliged to help you Own Your Home Years Sooner.

FACT 3: It is entirely up to you to take control of your home loan and find out all of the different strategies you can use to pay it off sooner.

On the other side of the counter, I would also like to address all those trusting souls who still insist on saying to me:

"If your Mortgage Elimination™ System is so good, then why hasn't my bank told me about it?"

Well, I hope that the facts I just outlined clarify this question and prove the only thing standing between you Owning Your Home Years Sooner, or being a slave to your home loan for the next 30 years, is your decision to empower yourself with, and apply, the knowledge in this book and on my website.

To give you an example, a friend asked me to examine her home loan because she wanted to know if she had the right type to help her reduce it quicker by applying my Mortgage Elimination™ System.

After reading this book, she went to her bank and was shocked to find that not only did they not tell her about a much better loan product that they had introduced nine months earlier, but that she was also paying 0.7% more interest on her existing home loan than she had to. Furthermore, they wanted to charge her $350 to transfer her loan to the new one.

What really impressed me was her attitude about the whole situation. She said to me, "I don't blame the banks because it's up to people like me to find out what's available and then take action."

As a result, she asked the right questions, got the new loan with the lower interest rate, and had the $350 administration fee waived as well. Consequently, she will now own her home 6 years earlier and save over $40,000 in interest.

A word of caution

Before you go on, it is important for you to immediately realize what this book is *not*.

First, it is not another dry, stuffy textbook about personal finance (as you are discovering). I want you to know that there is a real person who put this whole program together, and that's me. My name is Harj Gill, and I deal with *real* people, in the *real* world, and I want to communicate my ideas to you in a fun and relaxed way, as if you were sitting right across the table from me.

Second, this book is not about a 'get-rich-quick' scheme. There are plenty of scoundrels offering these in the world, but that's not what you will find in this book. However, if you...

✓ already have a Home Loan (normal Principle & Interest or a Home Equity Revolving Line of Credit), or,

✓ are a First-time Home Buyer looking for a loan, and . . .

. . . you want a simple, step-by-step, *foolproof* system to help you Own Your Home Years Sooner - and save tens of thousands of dollars in interest as well - then read on.

I also want to mention that *all* of the information in this book has grown out of my own experience and my consulting activities. Nearly all of the people I will refer to have saved at least $50,000 in interest on their home and investment loans (some much more).

I just want you to understand and appreciate the value of what you are holding in your hands. That's because it's equivalent to a personal consultation of at least $3,000 with me, and collectively represents hundreds of millions of dollars in interest savings by tens of thousands of people just like you. And, all that these people did was to make the decision to apply in their lives the simple Mortgage Elimination™ System I will share with you. If you diligently put into practice the information in this book and on my website, you too will Own Your Home Years Sooner.

Last, let me give you a brief outline of how I have organized this book so you know what to expect.

Part A: Why You Should Own Your Home Years Sooner – In this section, I summarize some of the major prevailing economic and global indicators that should have us all concerned. That's because they are very quickly putting home ownership out of reach of ordinary people. Also addressed are some of the issues that have led to people being complacent about NOT taking action to Own Their Homes Years Sooner, and why they should.

Part B: Learn How - Here I will present to you powerful knowledge about my Mortgage Elimination™ System.

Part C: Making It Work For You – In this section I will take you step-by-step through how to apply my system, so it works for you. I will cover the importance of having the right mental attributes and tools to Own Your Home Years Sooner. Also included in this section is getting the right type of loan to make my Mortgage Elimination™ System work effectively for you. In these loan chapters, I will describe what characteristics you should look for in the best loans, the pitfalls to avoid, and how to save time and money looking for the best one.

Part D: Things To Consider – This final part contains even more information that you will find helpful, such as how to save even more interest on your home loan, as well as a chapter for international readers.

So sit back and enjoy learning how to make your money work harder for you because this is definitely something your bank will not be running out the door to help you do!

"My banker asked me for a statement.
I said I was optimistic."

- Mark Victor Hansen -

"Don't let the opinions of the average person sway you. Dream, and they think you are crazy. Succeed, and they think you are lucky. Acquire wealth, and they think you are greedy. Pay no attention. They simply don't understand."

- Robert G. Allen -

Part A

Why You Should Own Your Home Years Sooner

*"A mortgage casts a shadow on
the sunniest fields."*

- R.G. Ingersoll -
(Illinois farmer, 1877)

"Experts with inflexible models ignore information that does not fit their models and tend to overvalue that which does fit."

- Donald Schön -

Chapter 1
Medicare and Social Security Facing Bankruptcy

"Don't let your schooling get in the way of your education."

- Mark Twain -

Although my obvious goal is to help you Own Your Home Years Sooner, my underlying purpose in developing this program has always been much more profound and subtle. You see, I want you to go way beyond Owning Your Home and become Financially Free as well.

Now why would I want you to do that?

Why do I want you to retire wealthy, or at least financially independent rather than simply stopping at paying off your mortgage?

The answer to this question should concern us all.

You see, most western industrialized nations have realized that their social security systems are not going to be able to support their ever-increasing aging populations in the near future.

For example, the Board of Trustees for the US Social Security System issued a press release on March 17, 2003* that read, *"Social Security is not Sustainable for the Long Term."*

In their annual report tabled at Congress, the trustees announced that there are only enough funds to sustain Social Security payments for another 39 years, and that Medicare will be completely bankrupt within the next 23 years. This means that Americans will no longer have access to Medicare by the year 2026 and no Social Security by 2042.

Now, there are two main reasons as to why this is happening.

First, the number of taxpayers in proportion to retired people is constantly diminishing because of lower fertility rates. Second, advancements in medical science are increasing the lifespan of those already here. Consequently, there are less and less people working to support more and more who are retiring.

Another way to look at all of this is that if you were 40 years old in 2003, then Medicare will be bankrupt by the time you are age 63, and you can no longer rely on Social Security after the age of 79. Therefore, you had better Own Your Home as soon as possible and begin an investment portfolio that can support you in your twilight years. Furthermore, if this information comes as a surprise to you, then I would encourage you to pass on this news to as many people as possible because they most likely don't know it either.

What's more, this social crisis is not unique to the US. You simply have to make the most simplistic inquiries into the state of the social welfare system in your country of residence, and you will find politicians facing a similar dilemma.

Now, in case this revelation doesn't set off a lot of alarm bells and is not sufficient to motivate you into taking action to Own Your Home Years Sooner because you are thinking, "I'm too young to even consider retirement, and by the time I get to that age, I'm sure all of this will be sorted out," I have some more bad news for you in the next chapter.

> *"It isn't what we don't know that gets us in trouble,*
> *it's what we know that ain't so."*
>
> *- David Stockman -*
> *(Former US Budget Director)*

*The 2003 Trustees Report can be viewed at:
www.socialsecurity.gov/OACT/TR/TR03/

Chapter 2

No Such Thing as Job Security

*"People and organizations frequently hold on to faulty
assumptions about their world for as long as a decade,
despite overwhelming evidence that it has changed
and they probably should too."*

- Andrew Pettigrew -

The status quo exists today whereby a lot of people are putting off Owning Their Homes Years Sooner because they have lulled themselves into a false sense of security. They have bought into the illusion that they are always going to have a job to make their mortgage repayments for the next twenty or thirty years. However, when compared to the evidence at hand, this is clearly a contradictory belief.

There are volumes of books written on this subject, so I will only present a summary of two of the main reasons as to why there is no such thing as "Job Security" anymore:

1.   Redundancy of information
2.   Globalization

1.   Redundancy of information

We are now well and truly in the "Information Age." Unfortunately, for most people, this does not extend beyond the thought of having their own access to the internet and cable TV. However, the repercussions of this paradigm shift go far beyond that.

For example, in 1988, scientific and technical information increased 13% per year, which meant that it doubled every 5.5 years. The rate has now jumped to over 40% per year because of new, more powerful information systems and an increasing population of scientists. That means that data now actually doubles every 20 months, and this growth continues to accelerate exponentially.

Furthermore, not only are we being swamped with information, but also the acceleration of unpredictable change makes some of our knowledge useless even before we get a hold of it. For example, the half-life of an engineer's knowledge in 1990 was five years. In other words, by 1995, it was predicted that only 50% of what an engineer knew in 1990 would still be relevant. In the field of Health, 85% of the information must now be upgraded every five years.

Consequently, a lot of people don't realize that a majority of what they originally studied to carry out their professions may no longer be relevant today. This holds true unless they have been engaged in a concerted effort to keep abreast of the latest developments in their field. However, most people can be forgiven for not doing this because of the fact that few have the time and energy to go to night classes and seminars after putting in a solid day's work. This is especially true for those raising a family.

2.   Globalization

Today's changes come at a much faster pace than our sociopolitical systems can handle. A televised press conference in London triggers an immediate reply in Berlin. An anonymous e-mail sent by a disgruntled employee causes share prices in a company to tumble. A change in the price of our dollar against the price of foreign currencies causes instantaneous purchases and sales in Sydney and Seattle. A politician's off-the-cuff remark about his or her foreign counterpart immediately results in calls for a downgrading of diplomatic and economic relations.

Increasingly, we cannot act independently because the repercussions are often felt interdependently. As industrialism has matured and world economies have become increasingly interconnected, decisions taken by a political and/or economic unit touch off effects outside of its own jurisdiction, thereby causing other political and commercial bodies to act in response. Thus, while one time people could make a decision without upsetting conditions outside of their own neatly defined areas of authority, this has become less and less possible.

Two recent classic examples, which clearly demonstrate the effect of globalization, are the war with Iraq and the SARS (Severe Acute Respiratory Syndrome) crisis.

As a direct result of SARS, airlines that were once profitable had their share prices slashed overnight, began losing millions of dollars a day, and laid off staff as the epidemic took its toll on flight bookings. Furthermore, Asian financial markets tumbled to new lows as the cost of SARS grew for the region's companies and economies.

According to Stephen Roach, Morgan Stanley's chief economist, the combination of a war and now a disease for which there is no known cure was knocking consumer and business confidence and slowing global growth. He went on to say we could expect a world recession in 2003 - after he previously forecast an annual growth of 2.5 per cent.

In case you think a world recession is not going to include you, let me paint a very quick scenario . . .

Let's say Mr. Roach's prediction does come true or some other unexpected global event takes place to bring it to fruition. This, by the way, was already starting to happen for one major US corporation whereby Starbucks shares fell 7% as investors worried that declining international growth would hinder the company's efforts to increase profit.

This decline in consumer confidence spreads to other industries and sectors as people no longer spend money on goods and services that they normally would. As a result, companies begin stockpiling surplus inventory in their warehouses because there is less demand for their products. The same goes for service industries, but their surplus comes in the form of unproductive staff waiting for the next appointment. These companies can only absorb the lack of cash flow for so long before they have to lay off staff. As a result, these newly unemployed add to the number of those who no longer have money to spend on goods and services, and that means there is even less money flowing into the economy. Now unless business and government institutions implement radical monetary and economic strategies to remedy this situation quickly, this downward spiral continues at the cost of tens of thousands of people being forced out of work, losing their homes, cars, businesses, and livelihoods.

We're in a recession

As of June 2003, unemployment in the US had hit a nine-year high of 6.1 %. There were predictions of a record projected US budget deficit of $US400 billion, a record trade deficit of $US500 billion, as well as a drifting US dollar which was fueling anxiety once again over the stalled US economy.

Furthermore, the Economic Policy Institute in Washington pointed to some bleak, long-term trends. It revealed that private sector jobs in the US had fallen by more than 3 million since the US recession began in March 2001, the largest private sector employment fall of any post-war recession.

"The US economy is in dire straits, undergoing a lengthy downturn, high unemployment, a fall in real wages, declining family incomes, and extensive job losses," the institute concluded.

What does all of this have to do with your mortgage?

The point I want to make is that we now live in extremely uncertain times and cannot easily predict what the future may hold.

So ask yourself these two questions:

- Are you so confident that the industry you work in is not going to be affected by events taking place on the other side of the world today?

- If you lost your job today, are your skills as current as those of the younger and hungrier who are graduating from college, and who will work for less money than you?

If you have fallen prey to a false sense of security and think that you will always be able to make your mortgage repayments for the next 30 years because you have a 'secure job', you may want to reassess that mindset because there is no such thing as job security anymore.

Before I help you to take that road to accelerated home ownership, there is one more fallacy we need to debunk because it keeps a lot of people from Owning Their Homes Years Sooner. This is the fallacy that a large mortgage has great tax benefits. In the next chapter, I'll put to rest this misconception.

"A desire to be in charge of our own lives,
a need for control, is born in each of us.
It is essential to our mental health, and
our success, that we take control"

- Robert F. Bennett -

Chapter 3

The Fallacy of a Mortgage Giving You a Tax Advantage

*"The greatest obstacle to discovery is not ignorance
- but the illusion of knowledge."*

- Daniel J. Boorstin -

One of the greatest and most tragic fallacies affecting millions of Americans is the belief that a large mortgage is an excellent wealth creation strategy. That's because those who are in such arrangements can deduct their interest payments and reduce their tax liability. I did not intend to include this topic in this book. However, I met an old acquaintance who is extremely intelligent, well educated, astute, and operates a very successful internet mail-order business, and his response to a question made me change my mind.

When he asked me what I was up to, I told him that I was revising my book to help global readers Own Their Homes Years Sooner. His retort was, "Harj, why would I want to do that when I get tax benefits by having a large mortgage?" He went on to say, "I have a good friend who is my financial advisor and whom I have known for many years, and I trust his judgement implicitly. This guy told me that the best thing for me to do tax wise is to keep my mortgage as large as possible for as long as possible."

I realized that this misconception is so ingrained in people's minds that even the most well intentioned 'advisors' have succumbed to it, and that I would have no choice but to address the issue. So here we go . . .

By the way, I'm not saying that you should discount how you structure your finances to maximize tax benefits. However, trying to do so with a large mortgage just doesn't make any sense, as you will see in the compelling example I have put forward.

Incidentally, I used the data from the Tax Rate Schedule in the IRS 2002-1040 booklet as a guide to demonstrate my point. I'll create a hypothetical case example where two single individuals are filing their tax returns. Furthermore, we are going to make the assumption that the circumstances for both individuals are exactly the same, except Person A does not have a mortgage and Person B does. Now, let's have a look at the taxable and disposable incomes each person has before and after taxes.

	Person A	Person B
Gross Income	$65,000	$65,000
Mortgage	No	Yes
Interest on Mortgage	Nil	$11,567
Taxable Income	$65,000	$53,433
Total Tax Paid	$13,896	$10,773
Difference in taxes paid	+$3,123	
Total Disposable Income	$51,104	$42,660
Monetary Advantage	**+ $8,444**	

As you can see, Person A paid $3,123 ($13,896 - $10,773) more in taxes than Person B, but still had $8,444 ($51,104 - $42,660) more in their pocket than their counterpart who has a mortgage and who received a 'tax benefit' of $11,567!

How can this be, you ask?

Well, for every dollar Person B paid to the bank in interest, he received 27 cents back in tax savings. Alternatively, Person A, who didn't have a mortgage and didn't have any interest to claim as a deduction, still had the $11,567 as part of their taxable income.

Consequently, Person A paid 27 cents on the dollar to the government on this amount instead and kept the remainder. The end result is that he had $8,444 more to spend than Person B.

If you don't believe me, take out your 2002 tax schedules, do these calculations, and then take them to your tax attorney for verification. I hope this lays to rest once and for all this horrendous misconception that has been perpetrated, and perpetuated, on the American public for far too long.

 HOT TIP

> If getting 27 cents back on the dollar makes sense to you, then I have a much better offer. Send me as many dollars as you like, and I will send back to you 50 cents for every dollar!

But that will never happen here!

Remember in Chapter 1, I referred to the 2003 report to Congress from the Board of Trustees of the US Social Security System? Three of the points they went on to make in that report were:

- "The projected point at which tax revenues will fall below program costs comes in 2018."

- "Today, there are 3.3 workers paying Social Security payroll taxes for every one person collecting Social Security benefits. That number will drop to 2-to-1 in less than 40 years. <u>At this ratio there will not be enough workers to pay scheduled benefits at current tax rates</u>."

- "As stated in the Trustees Report, <u>the sooner we address the problem, the less abrupt the changes will have to be</u>."

I want you to take particular note of the underlined text, and put yourself in the shoes of the policy makers for a moment.

What options do you think you would have to exercise in order to take care of your ever-increasing number of retiring constituents? One option may be to increase Medicare and Social Security tax rates to make up for the projected shortfall. Another may be to decrease the amount paid to Social Security recipients. What about either reducing or completely abolishing the tax deductibility of interest on home loans and using that as an added revenue stream to fund these programs?

Think it won't happen?

 NEWS FLASH

Testimony of Chairman Alan Greenspan
Economic outlook and current fiscal issues
Before the Committee on the Budget, U.S. House of Representatives
February 25, 2004

In a testimony before the House Budget Committee, Federal Reserve Chairman, Alan Greenspan, said that the current deficit situation, a projected record of $521 billion this year, will worsen dramatically once the baby boom generation starts becoming eligible for Social Security benefits in just four years. Greenspan went on to urge Congress to deal with this situation by cutting benefits for future Social Security retirees rather than raising taxes.

"This dramatic demographic change is certain to place enormous demands on our nation's resources - demands we will almost surely be unable to meet unless action is taken," Greenspan said. "For a variety of reasons, that action is better taken as soon as possible."

To view the full 2004 Testimony of Chairman Greenspan, go to http://www.federalreserve.gov/boarddocs/testimony/2004/200402 25/default.htm

If you look at history, you will find that desperate situations often lead bureaucrats to take desperate measures, and the Medicare and Social Security forecasts are one of those extremely desperate situations facing this country. These forecasts are not hypothetical, my friends. They are facts that need to be taken very, very seriously by everyone.

As I always say, rather than blame others when it's too late, it is a most wise person who takes control of their own destiny - NOW!

Having said that, imagine how different your thinking processes will be when you Own Your Home. In fact, why don't you take a moment to ponder that right now before I share with you how it all works in the next section?

"There are three types of people in the world:
Those who make things happen,
Those who watch things happen, and
Those who wonder what happened."

- Dan Kennedy -

Part B

Learn How (Step 1)

*"The significant problems we face cannot be solved
at the same level of thinking we were at
when we created them."*

- Albert Einstein -

*"The grand essentials of happiness are;
something to do,
something to love, and,
something to hope for."*

- Allan K. Chalmers -

The Mortgage Elimination™ System

I want to begin this part of the book by saying:

To Own Your Home Years Sooner, YOU DON'T have to be a financial genius, or have tons of money.

This is perhaps the most important point I want to communicate to you in this book.

Over the past eight years, I have refined my Mortgage Elimination™ System through the process of listening to readers like you who have given me invaluable feedback, so that it is easy to understand and even easier to apply. The only obstacle now seems to be that people can't believe how simple it all is – especially when they see how much money they will save. For example, I received the following response from one reader I met:

> *"I borrowed your book from a colleague at work, got inspired and then tried to explain your Mortgage Elimination™ System to my wife.*
>
> *"You're right. At first, she was very skeptical and thought it too good to be true. But after trying for several months, I simply got my own copy and said to her, 'just read this'.*
>
> *"The result led to both of us racing out the door to take action...and now we are well on our way to owning our home a lot sooner than we had dreamt possible!"*

I'm sure that once you start using my Mortgage Elimination™ System, you too will be surprised at just how quickly you will start achieving *results* – and that's my definition of real success. As far as I am concerned, everything else is just hype.

Again, to alleviate your concerns about the legitimacy of this system, I'd like to remind you that the Australian subsidiary of HSBC Bank, one of the largest banks in the world, created a home loan for that country based on the guidelines I recommend in my book. Furthermore, they used the Australian edition of my book to promote their new home loan in that country. This was only done after the book, and this system, were stringently assessed by the bank's legal department for several months. See Appendix 1 for the full-page HSBC Bank advertisement that ran in major newspapers in that country.

Moving right along, here are the three simple steps to my Mortgage Elimination™ System:

1. Learn How
2. Get The Right Loan
3. Create Your Plan

As you read on, you will see how each of these steps fit in the sequence, and why (international readers please refer to Chapter 19).

In this part of the book I will share with you the first step, which is all about the secret as to why traditional loans take so long to pay off. But more importantly, I show you how to take advantage of that fact to Own Your Home Years Sooner and save thousands of dollars in interest on your home loan.

To do this, I will use some simple calculations and figures from real life case studies encountered during my consulting days. You may note that some of the loan amounts in the examples will seem rather paltry, and the incomes of the people concerned certainly do not put them in the mega-rich category. I have deliberately selected these case examples to make the point that ordinary people are using my Mortgage Elimination™ System to Own Their Homes Years Sooner.

As a side note, according to Thomas Stanley and William Danko[1], 80% of America's millionaires are first-generation rich, which means they made their money on their own, and 97% of them are homeowners. How do you think they got to be where they are? Stanley and Danko go on to say, one of the most important factors that led these people to becoming rich is that "they allocate their time, energy, and money efficiently, in ways conducive to building wealth."

I can tell you from personal experience that those people who have diligently applied my Mortgage Elimination™ System have joined the ranks of the financially free. For example, Nick and Christine, a couple who started this program in 1995, completely Owned Their Home by August 2000, saved over $97,000 in interest, and were on their way to owning their third investment property at that time. If you would like to see this couple being interviewed on a national current affairs program, visit my website. Meanwhile, let's get you started as well!

---

[1] Stanley, T.J. and W.D. Danko. 1996. *The Millionaire Next Door*. Harper*Business* Publishers.

Chapter 4
The Key to Owning Your Home Years Sooner

"If you're heading in the right direction,
each step, no matter how small, is
getting you closer to your goal."

- Jackson Brown -

 KEY PRINCIPLE

Interest on your loan is calculated on the daily balance and charged at the end of the month (called 'monthly in arrears').

When your bank calculates the interest payments on your home loan, they usually work it out on the daily balance of your loan and *usually* charge you that interest at the end of the month (called 'monthly in arrears').

That's it!

The whole secret to paying off your home or investment loan years sooner hinges on understanding and taking advantage of this Key Principle. The best way to begin is by examining what you and most people are doing now.

Please note the information and case studies to follow apply equally well to people who have any other loan that is secured against a property.

The traditional 'P&I' Loan

The type of home loan most commonly offered by the banks is referred to as a 'Principal & Interest (P&I) Loan'. That's because you are not only paying interest on the money you borrowed, but you are also reducing the 'Principal' (the amount borrowed) - albeit v-e-r-y s-l-o-o-o-w-l-y. Let's look at why that is through a simple illustration.

Case Example - Martin & Genevieve

This couple had a $100,000 home loan at 10% interest. The bank told them if they made repayments of $908.70 per month, it would take them 25 years to pay off their loan.

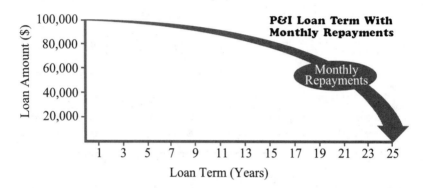

PROFILE

LOAN AMOUNT:	$100,000
INTEREST RATE:	10%
LOAN TERM:	25 years
FREQUENCY OF PAYMENTS:	Monthly
PAYMENT AMOUNT:	$908.70 per month

The way interest is calculated

Remember our Key Principle: interest is calculated on the daily balance of your home loan and charged monthly in arrears.

Martin and Genevieve started their loan in January owing $100,000, and because they were making monthly repayments, their daily balance remained at $100,000 for each day of January until they made their next repayment (on the last day of January). That's because most lenders calculate the interest payable for a full month and then charge you that interest at the end of the month.

On the next page are the daily balances for the first 4 months of Martin and Genevieve's $100,000 loan and the daily interest charged for each of those 4 months.

Month	Daily Balance	Daily Interest Charged
Jan	$100,000.00	$27.40
Feb	$99,940.70	$27.38
Mar	$99,798.64	$27.34
Apr	$99,737.48	$27.32

Here's the formula the banks use to work out the amount of daily interest charged:

$$Daily\ Interest = \frac{Loan\ Amount \times Interest\ Rate}{365\ days}$$

The amount of interest charged varies each month

We know that not all months have the same number of days. So in order to calculate the interest that would be charged for each month, we would have to multiply the daily interest amount by the number of days in that month.

Monthly Interest = Daily Interest x Number of Days in Month

Consequently, the interest charged for Martin and Genevieve's Loan for the Month of January was:

Interest Charged (Jan) = $27.40 x 31 days = $849.40

Now that we know the amount of interest this couple paid in January ($849.40), what happened when they made their first repayment of $908.70?

Jan 1	Opening Balance	$100,000.00
Jan 31	Loan Repayment	- $908.70
	Interest Charged (Jan)	+ $849.40
	Closing Balance (End of Jan)	= $99,940.70

As you can see, the amount of interest charged for the month of January ($849.40) was less than Martin and Genevieve's monthly repayment ($908.70).

This means that after the first month's repayment was made, a portion of the principal was reduced to give them a Closing Balance for January. This then became the Opening Balance for the month of February, and the whole process started all over again. Note: although they made a loan repayment of $908.70, they reduced the principal *by only $59.30*.

Here's what happened in February:

Daily Interest = $\dfrac{(\$99,940.70 \times 10\%)}{365 \text{ days}}$ = $27.38

Therefore, the interest charged for the Month of February was:

Interest Charged (Feb) = $27.38 x 28 days = $766.64

Feb 1	Opening Balance	$99,940.70
Feb 28	Loan Repayment	- $908.70
	Interest Charged (Feb)	+ $766.64
	Closing Balance (End of Feb)	= $99,798.64

After two months and having paid a total of $1,817.40 toward their mortgage, Martin and Genevieve reduced their loan by just $201.36.

Let's take a look at the daily balances for the first 4 months of Martin and Genevieve's $100,000 loan and the daily and monthly interest charged for each of those 4 months:

Month	Daily Balances	Daily Interest Charged	Monthly Interest
Jan	$100,000.00	$27.40 (x 31 days)	= $849.40
Feb	$99,940.70	$27.38 (x 28 days)	= $766.64
Mar	$99,798.64	$27.34 (x 31 days)	= $847.54
Apr	$99,737.48	$27.32 (x 30 days)	= $819.60

As you can see, the daily balances for the loan decreased each month (i.e., from $100,000 in January to $99,737.48 in April), and as a result, the daily interest charged also decreased (i.e., from $27.40 in January to $27.32 in

April). If you look carefully at the daily interest charged, you will notice that there is a decrease in daily interest of only 8¢ a day after four months. Doesn't sound like much, does it? But these pennies add up to tens of thousands of dollars in interest payments over the term of the loan because of compound interest – and this interest cost is what I'm going to show you how to reduce by using my Mortgage Elimination™ System.

Meanwhile, if Martin and Genevieve's loan repayments stayed at $908.70 per month (assuming the interest rate also stayed at 10%), more and more of their repayment would have gone toward reducing their loan as time went by.

However, as with most 25 year P&I loans, a large part of their repayments would have gone toward paying the interest on their loan in the first 10 to 15 years, with only a small portion actually reducing the principal.

"Never stand begging for
what you have the power to earn."

- Miguel de Cervantes -

Summary

KEY PRINCIPLE

Interest on your loan is calculated on the daily balance and charged at the end of the month (called 'monthly in arrears').

The most important point to emphasize here is that interest on your home loan is calculated on the daily balance and *usually* charged monthly in arrears. And if you are making periodic repayments (i.e., monthly, bi-weekly, or, weekly), the daily balance of your home loan stays the same until the next repayment is made.

Now, if there was a way to reduce the daily balance of your home loan, then obviously this would reduce the amount of interest you would have to pay and also reduce the term of the loan (this will be explained in much more detail in the chapters to follow).

Incidentally, the couple from this chapter paid off their original $100,000, 25 year home loan in just under 5 years by creating and implementing their own Mortgage Elimination™ Plan, as I will show you how to do.

"Cherish your visions and your dreams as they
are the children of your soul, the blueprints
of your ultimate achievements."

- Napoleon Hill -

Chapter 5

Outdated Methods of Loan Reduction

*"If the rhythm of the drum beat changes,
the dance step must adapt."*

- West African proverb -

In the last chapter we saw Martin and Genevieve using a traditional P&I loan to make monthly repayments, which would have taken them 25 years to pay off. That's because over the first 10 to 15 years of a typical 25 year P&I loan, most of the repayments go toward paying the interest on the loan while only a small portion actually reduces the principal.

The table below shows the End of Year Balances for a $100,000 home loan (with monthly repayments of $908.70 per month) at an interest rate of 10%:

Year	Total Payments	Principal Paid	Interest Paid	Mortgage Balance
1	$10,904	$947	$9,957	$99,053
2	$21,809	$1,993	$19,816	$98,007
3	$32,713	$3,149	$29,564	$96,851
5	$54,522	$5,836	$48,686	$94,164
10	$109,044	$15,438	$93,606	$84,562
15	$163,566	$31,237	$132,329	$68,763
25	$272,611	$100,000	$172,611	$0

After 15 years, a total of $163,566 worth of repayments would have been made with only $31,237 of the principal being reduced.

The situation I have just described is not uncommon. What's more, many people think that there's not much they can do about accelerating the reduction of their home loan - other than engaging in one of the following outdated methods. . .

Paying Bi-weekly

You probably know by now that paying bi-weekly rather than monthly will cut years off your home loan. The way it works is as follows:

Example: Home loan of $100,000 at 10% interest over 25 years with monthly repayments of $908.70. This means that you will be making 12 equal sized repayments of $908.70 each year.

i.e., $908.70 x 12 months = $10,904.40

However, if you choose to divide this monthly figure in half and pay bi-weekly, this is the result:

$454.35 x 26 bi-weekly payments = $11,813.10

If you compare the figures for the two repayment methods, you get a difference of $908.70.

i.e., $11,813.10 - $10,904.40 = $908.70 = 1 month's extra repayment

So you can see that by dividing the original monthly repayment in half and paying this amount bi-weekly, you will actually make one extra month's repayment per year (in this case an extra $908.70 per year - which will reduce the term of this P&I loan from 25 years down to 18 years and 6 months).

Example: Servicing a mortgage of $100,000 at 10% interest with bi-weekly repayments of $454.35 would result in the following End of Year Balances:

Year	Total Payments	Principal Paid	Interest Paid	Mortgage Balance
1	$11,813	$1,926	$9,887	$98,074
2	$23,626	$4,054	$19,572	$95,946
3	$35,439	$6,405	$29,034	$93,595
5	$59,066	$11,871	$47,195	$88,129
10	$118,131	$31,402	$86,729	$68,598
15	$177,196	$63,537	$113,660	$36,463
19	$220,866	$100,000	$120,866	$0

After 15 years, a total of $177,196 worth of repayments would have been made with $63,537 of the principal being decreased - more than double the reduction when compared to our original monthly repayment method!

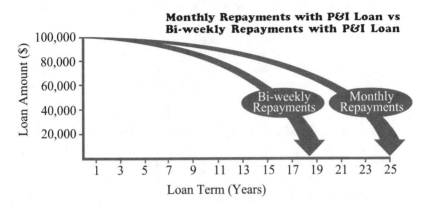

Monthly Repayments with P&I Loan vs Bi-weekly Repayments with P&I Loan

Below is the end of year balance comparisons for both the monthly and the bi-weekly repayment methods:

Year	Principal Owed (Monthly Payment)	Principal Owed (Bi-weekly Payment)
1	$99,053	$98,074
2	$98,007	$95,946
3	$96,851	$93,595
5	$94,164	$88,129
10	$84,562	$68,598
15	$68,763	$36,463
19	$49,051	$0

In effect, the bi-weekly repayment method would reduce the $100,000 loan at 10% interest from 25 years down to 18 years 6 months and result in an interest saving of $51,745.

INSIDER SECRET

What I have described in terms of saving time and interest by making bi-weekly payments is not that difficult to do through simple negotiations with your current lender (if they offer this option).

However, the most disturbing aspect I have found in the United States is the number of 'advisors' and 'consultants' who are offering to set up this type of 'accelerated mortgage reduction plan' for you for a 'small investment' (usually around $400) - without disclosing their true methodology.

For example, I came across one program where the company will collect the money from you on a bi-weekly basis, but through slight of hand, don't exactly offer you the bi-weekly interest benefits.

Here's how this particular scheme worked. . .

Imagine you were making $1,000 a month in repayments to your lender, which equates to $12,000 per year in repayments.

You now switch to this company's 'accelerated mortgage reduction program' and make bi-weekly repayments of $500 to them, which totals $13,000 a year (i.e., $500 x 26 payments).

The company actually keeps making $1,000 a month in repayments to your lender for 11 months, and then makes a single $2,000 payment at the end of the year, so it equates to a total of $13,000 in repayments over 12 months.

Here's the catch. Although your loan term will still be reduced because of the extra repayment being made AT THE END of each year, you DO NOT actually receive the full interest benefit of the bi-weekly repayment method. That's because this company pockets the interest on the money not immediately paid to your lender. Now if you have tens of thousands (if not millions) of clients on your books, you can imagine the substantial returns this company is making from scamming ordinary people like you.

The bottom line is, don't spend your money on this type of program because there are much more effective ways to Own Your Home Years Sooner - without making extra interest payments, and I will share them with you in this book.

Paying weekly

Contrary to what some people may think, paying weekly instead of bi-weekly won't reduce the term of your home loan a great deal. The reason again is that you won't make any extra payments each year.

This can be illustrated by using our previous example of a $100,000 loan at 10% interest again.

I said that if you made 12 equal sized monthly repayments of $908.70 each year, you would pay $10,904.40 per year toward your home loan:

i.e., $908.70 x 12 months = $10,904.40

Again, if you choose to divide this monthly figure ($908.70) in half and pay bi-weekly, this is the result:

$454.35 x 26 bi-weekly repayments = $11,813.10

And if you compare the figures for both repayment methods, you get a difference of $908.70 - which equates to one extra month's repayment per year - which is the reason the term of the loan is reduced so substantially.

i.e., $11,813.10 - $10,904.40 = $908.70 = 1 month's extra repayment

Now, if you divide this bi-weekly figure ($454.35) in half again to make weekly repayments, this is the result:

$227.175 x 52 weeks = $11,813.10

You can see that by paying weekly rather than bi-weekly, you won't actually make any extra repayments because there are still only 52 weeks in a year. However, you would reduce the loan term from 18 years 6 months to 18 years 5 months because the daily balance is reduced weekly rather than bi-weekly.

Making lump sum payments

Another common method of accelerating loan reduction familiar to most people is to make lump sum payments toward their P&I Loan. For example, let's say you get a tax refund of $2,000 and you decide to put this toward your $100,000 home loan in July of the first year.

What would happen is that the daily balance for July would be reduced by an extra $2,000, and this would shorten the overall term of your $100,000 loan from 25 years to 23 years, and save you $18,750 in interest (based on the monthly repayment method).

If you were paying bi-weekly instead of monthly, and you injected this $2,000 into the loan, you would reduce the loan term from 18 years 6 months to 17 years 3 months and save $9,474 in interest.

Increasing your repayments

Of course, increasing the amount of your repayments will also reduce the daily balance every month (or bi-weekly) and cut the loan term.

Example: $100,000 loan at 10% interest with repayments of $454.35 paid bi-weekly.

If you were to increase your repayments by $20 to $474.35 bi-weekly, you would reduce the loan from 18 years 6 months to 16 years 5 months and save $15,835 in interest.

After emphasizing the Key Principle and exploring traditional methods of accelerating loan repayments, the conclusion one naturally reaches is that there is no way to reduce your home loan unless you make extra repayments or happen to come across a windfall and make a Lump Sum Payment toward your P&I Loan.

But that's where taking advantage of the Key Principle and some of the specialized loans available through the banking system can help you, and we will explore these next.

"The willingness to do whatever it takes is infinitely more important than knowing everything there is to know about how to do it."

- Jamieson Squire Poignand -

Summary

The traditional, outdated methods of accelerating loan reduction familiar to most people are:

1. Making bi-weekly repayments;
2. Making weekly repayments;
3. Making lump sum repayments;
4. Increasing your repayments.

These traditional methods of accelerating debt reduction do serve to reduce the term of a loan and consequently save you interest. However, we will now explore a repayment method that tens of thousands of ordinary people are using all over the world to achieve spectacular results in Owning Their Homes Years Sooner – without making extra interest payments.

> *"If you do what you've always done,*
> *you'll get what you've always gotten."*
>
> *- Linda Coleman-Willis -*

"Make it a must that whenever you hear about something, read, or research something you think has value for your Life, don't let it become just knowledge. Convert it into action; for it is through our actions that our destiny is shaped."

- Anthony Robbins -

Chapter 6

Using the Key Principle to Own Your Home Years Sooner and Save $1,000s in Interest

*"If you focus on the problem, you can't see the solution.
See what no one else sees. See what everyone else chooses
not to see out of fear, conformity, and laziness."*

- Patch Adams -

Getting ahead financially

If you want to improve your financial position in life, there are really only two main ways to do it:

1. Work harder to earn extra money, or

2. Work smarter and make more effective and efficient use of your existing financial resources.

It's the second of these options that I will show you how to apply in order to Own Your Home Years Sooner by using my Mortgage Elimination™ System.

The following is a real life case example showing how an ordinary couple learned to work smarter to reduce the term of their home loan and will save over $90,000 in interest in the process.

Case Study - Bill & Greta

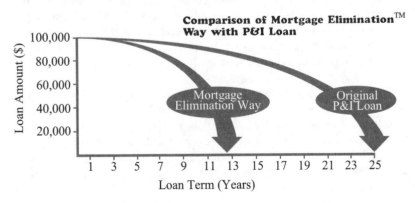

Comparison of Mortgage Elimination™ Way with P&I Loan

PROFILE

LOAN AMOUNT:	$100,000
INCOME:	$39,000 per year
LOAN TERM:	Reduced from 25 years down to 12 years 7 months
INTEREST SAVINGS:	$93,773

Bill & Greta started with the same $100,000 loan amount as Martin and Genevieve from Chapter 4. Their repayments were also the same (i.e., $908.70 per month).

However, Bill and Greta used the Key Principle outlined in this book to reduce their home loan from 25 years down to 12 years 7 months and will save $93,773 in interest.

Bill was a diesel mechanic in his forties, on an income of $32,000 per annum, and his wife Greta worked part time and earned $7,000 per year. As you can see, we're not talking about high rollers here. These are ordinary people whom you would call the 'salt of the Earth'.

Their lender had told them that their existing home loan of $100,000 would take them nearly 25 years to pay off.

Their last home loan statement showed that they had only reduced their home loan by $1,127 in the previous 12 months, *even though* they had paid a total of $11,572 in repayments to the bank. This was a situation with which they were totally fed up with and wanted to improve upon.

To do this, Bill considered working away from home in a mine because he could earn more money there, and Greta thought about getting a full time job. These prospects neither of them desired because they had two young children to take care of, and they wanted to bring them up jointly, not with one parent being away for most of the year. In other words, like many people, they felt they had to work harder to earn extra money, in order to make extra payments on their home loan to pay it off sooner.

However, by taking advantage of the Key Principle in this book and making more effective and efficient use of their existing financial resources, they were well on their way to Owning Their Home Years Sooner – without making extra interest payments. Furthermore, they did this without having to change their existing lifestyle – a lifestyle with which they were very happy. Let me share with you what they did to improve their situation . . .

The old way of making repayments

In order to service their original Principal and Interest loan, Bill & Greta – like most people – had structured their finances in the following manner:

1. Bill & Greta's income went into a checking/savings account.

2. At the end of each month they wrote a check to their lender from their checking account to service their home loan.

3. The amount left in the checking/savings account was then used for living expenses and the rest of the money stayed in their account for 'emergency' use (see diagram below).

Sounds familiar, doesn't it?

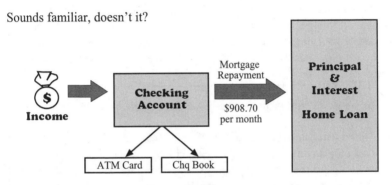

If you are making your home loan repayments in the same way as Bill & Greta once did, then you are not making the most efficient use of your money. That's because the money that sits in your checking/savings account for living expenses and emergency use is 'dead' money, as it earns nil to very little interest (around 0% - 2%), which in turn is taxed at your marginal tax rate.

The new way of making repayments

Bill & Greta wanted to work smarter, not harder. So, they applied my Mortgage Elimination™ System and refinanced to a type of loan that maximized our Key Principle to their advantage. Consequently, they changed their repayment structure from a 'Principal and Interest' (P&I) loan to a 'Home Equity Line of Credit' (also known as a HELOC type of loan).

This type of loan enabled them to have all of their income paid directly into their home loan, thus having the effect of immediately reducing their loan by the amount of income that went into it. It also gave them the flexibility to withdraw their money 'at call' without incurring any costs. Basically, I am talking about turning a home loan into a day-to-day transaction account with an ATM card and checkbook access.

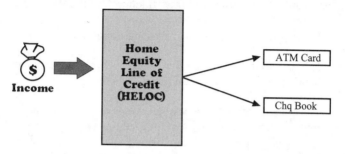

When used in conjunction with a personalized Mortgage Elimination™ Plan, which is an integral part of my system, this method can drastically shorten the term of your home loan. That's because every cent you deposit into your home loan now works to save you interest by reducing your daily balance.

 HOT TIP

SAVING interest is the same as EARNING interest – except it's better!

When Bill and Greta had their surplus funds sitting in their checking/savings account, they earned 1.35% interest on these funds, which were then taxed at their marginal tax rate. When they started depositing these funds into their HELOC instead, they began to save 10% in interest on the equivalent amount on their home loan – and they did not have to pay any tax because they were saving interest instead of earning interest.

I really want to emphasize this point, so I'm going to use an example to illustrate what I mean.

Let's say Bill and Greta had $2,000 in their checking/savings account, which they had accumulated for a vacation. This $2,000 was earning them 1.35% in interest, which they had to pay tax on at their marginal tax rate.

By transferring that $2,000 into their HELOC until they need it, they will reduce their loan by this amount of money. This means they would now save interest at the rate of 10% on $2,000 of their HELOC, which is really the same as earning 10% on the $2,000 that was previously sitting in their checking/savings account. The best part is, they don't have to pay any tax on this increased 'return' because they are saving interest as opposed to earning interest.

Are you beginning to see the interest benefits if you also have all of your income and any surplus funds sitting in your HELOC until these funds are needed?

Let's move on now and look at how Bill & Greta's decision to use the Mortgage Elimination™ System worked for them.

STEP 1

Jan 1	Mortgage Owing	$100,000
2	Income Deposited	-$1,200
	Mortgage Balance	= $98,800

Bill & Greta took out a HELOC (Home Equity Line of Credit) on the 1st of January for $100,000 at an interest rate of 10%. Immediately, they put their bi-weekly income of $1,200 into the home loan, which reduced it down to $98,800. Remember our Key Principle: interest is calculated on the daily balance. So from that point on, until they withdrew any money, the interest was calculated on the daily balance of $98,800.

STEP 2

Jan 2	Mortgage Owing	$100,000
	Income Deposited	-$1,200
	Mortgage Balance	= $98,800

Jan 3	Withdraw Budgeted Weekly Expenses	+$270
	Mortgage Balance	= $99,070

On the 3rd of January, they withdrew $270 for their weekly budgeted expenses in accordance with their Mortgage Elimination™ Plan, and their Home Loan Balance increased to $99,070 – interest was now calculated on this daily balance.

Notice that each time they withdrew money from their home loan, it increased the amount they owed, and whenever they deposited money into their home loan, it decreased the amount they owed.

STEP 3

Jan 3	Mortgage Balance	$99,070
10	Withdraw Budgeted Weekly	+270
	Mortgage Balance	= $99,340
Jan 16	Income Deposited	-$1,200
	Mortgage Balance	= $98,140

On the 10th of January, they once again withdrew their budgeted weekly expenses of $270, which increased the home loan to $99,340. On the 16th of January, their regular bi-weekly income of $1,200 was deposited into the home loan, which reduced it to $98,140 – and the interest was calculated on this daily balance until the next transaction took place.

STEP 4

Jan 16	Mortgage Balance	$98,140
17	Withdraw Weekly Expenses	+$270
	Mortgage Balance	= $98,410
Jan 24	Withdraw Weekly Expenses	+$270
30	Withdraw Money for Bills	+$250
	Income Deposited	-$1,200
	Mortgage Balance	= $97,730
Jan 31	Mortgage Balance	= $97,730
	Withdraw Weekly Expenses	+$270
	Interest Deducted	+$839
	Mortgage Balance	+ $98,839

The process of income going in and expenses coming out of their new loan continued until the end of the month when the bank deducted $839 in interest from Bill and Greta's HELOC.

At this stage, I need to point out some major characteristics of this type of loan.

First, you are only required to make the interest payments on a HELOC, which is calculated on the fluctuating daily balances throughout each month. This is unlike a P&I Loan where you are required to make set, regular repayments.

Second, it is the surplus funds left in the HELOC, which reduce the principal of the loan. As you can see, this couple decreased the principal of their loan by $1,161 after only the first month – remember on the 1st of January they owed $100,000, but by the 31st of January they owed $98,839.

This $1,161 'reduction' at the end of January was achieved by having all of their income deposited into their HELOC, only withdrawing budgeted living expenses in accordance with their Mortgage Elimination™ Plan, and leaving all of their surplus income in the loan. These funds, instead of sitting in their checking/savings account earning them 1.35% interest, were now working much harder for them by reducing the interest payable on their home loan at the rate of 10% - *tax free!* Remember saving interest is equivalent to earning interest.

Again, here is what happened in January:

Total Income:	$3,600
Total Budgeted Living Expenses:	- $1,600
Interest Deducted:	- $839
Surplus Income for January:	+ $1,161

Therefore, $100,000 - $1,161 = $98,839 (the HELOC balance at the end of January).

Let's have a look at what happened in the second month (February).

February

Feb 1	Mortgage Balance	$98,839
7	Withdraw Weekly Expenses	+$270
	Mortgage Balance	= $99,109
Feb 13	Income Deposited	- $1,200
	Mortgage Balance	= $97,909
Feb 14	Withdraw Weekly Expenses	+ $270
	Mortgage Balance	= $98,179
Feb 21	Withdraw Weekly Expenses	+ $270
	Mortgage Balance	= $98,449
Feb 27	Income Deposited	- $1,200
	Mortgage Balance	= $97,249
Feb 28	Mortgage Balance	= $97,249
	Withdraw Money for Bills	+ $239
	Interest Deducted	+ $755
	Mortgage Balance	= $98,243

As you can see, by the end of the second month this couple had reduced their loan by $1,757 - that's more than they had been able to achieve in the *entire previous year!* What's more, they had not changed their lifestyle and were still living on the same amount of money to which they had become accustomed.

Although I have only shown the budget for the first two months for Bill & Greta, their outgoings did fluctuate due to periodic expenses, such as bills for electricity, telephone, gas, etc. This is where having the right tool (i.e., software program) comes in very handy because it allows you to take into account fluctuating expense items and stay on track with your projected loan term.

By switching over to my Mortgage Elimination™ System and using a HELOC, Bill and Greta reduced their 25 year P&I loan down to 12 years 7 months and will save $93,773 in interest – all without significantly changing their existing lifestyle.

Below is a comparison of their original P&I loan repayment method with the Mortgage Elimination™ Way.

Comparison of Original P&I Loan with Mortgage Elimination™ Way		
After Year	Loan Balance (Original P&I)	Loan Balance (HELOC)
1	$99,053	$97,150
2	$98,007	$93,682
3	$96,851	$89,516
4	$95,574	$84,566
5	$94,164	$78,738
6	$92,606	$72,011
7	$90,894	$64,336
8	$88,983	$55,604
9	$86,882	$45,694
10	$84,562	$34,473
11	$81,998	$21,791
12	$79,166	$7,494
13	**$76,037**	**$0**

As you can see, if they kept going the way they were, it would have taken them another 12 years to pay off their P&I loan.

 HOT TIP

The amount by which your home loan is reduced using this repayment method depends on three things:

1. The size of your home loan, which dictates the amount of interest you are charged each month.
2. The size of your income.
3. Your personal expenses and how often you withdraw them.

The key to saving money is that interest is calculated on the daily balance of your home loan and charged monthly in arrears. So what you want to aim for is having as much money as you can sitting in your home loan for as long as you can, thereby reducing the amount of interest you have to pay.

However, even if you were to spend all of your surplus funds and only leave in the HELOC the repayment amount you currently make toward your existing P&I loan, you will still pay your home loan off sooner and save interest using this approach. That's because for the days that you have not withdrawn all of your money, the interest charged is less. Even leaving your money in the HELOC for just a few days each month can have an effect of saving you interest and reducing the overall term of your home loan because of the magic of compound interest.

 HOT TIP

Before you rush off and refinance, I want you to know that a 'Home Equity Line of Credit' (HELOC) is not the same as a 'Home Equity Loan'. Furthermore, although most lenders are offering HELOCs in one form or another, not all of them have HELOCs with the appropriate features to make my Mortgage Elimination™ System work effectively. At this stage, I don't want you to worry about this because I will explain it all in more detail in Part C, 'Making It Work For You.' All I want you to focus on right now is getting the Key Principle thoroughly ingrained in your psyhe.

A word about 'Equity'

The type of loan I described in this chapter is called a 'HELOC' because it allows you to borrow against the equity in your home – the percentage of your home that you actually own. For example, if your home is worth $100,000 and you still owe the bank $70,000, then you have $30,000 (30%) equity in your home.

Knowing the amount of equity you have in your home is important because, in most cases to qualify for a HELOC, you must have at least 10% equity in your home. Having said that, since the last printing of this book, I have sourced lenders who are willing to relax this criteria so you can get started with my system ASAP - more on this in Part C.

Summary

There are two ways to get ahead in life: work harder or work smarter. Unfortunately, most people think that the only way to pay off their home or investment loans sooner is to work harder.

However, there are now certain types of home loans available that enable you to have your money work harder for you instead, thereby allowing you to cut years off of your home loan and save tens of thousands of dollars in interest.

These loans are commonly called Home Equity Lines of Credit, or HELOCs for short. They enable you to deposit all of your income into your home loan and to withdraw your living expenses as required, at call.

In effect, this transforms your home loan into a day-to-day transaction account, enabling you to take full advantage of our Key Principle. That's because now, every dollar that is left in the home loan reduces the daily balance of your loan, thereby reducing the amount of interest you are charged.

In the remaining chapters of this section, I will take you through a number of different case studies that build your knowledge on how this type of loan has been used by tens of thousands of people to Own Their Homes Years Sooner – without making extra interest payments.

> *"One can't believe impossible things," said Alice.*
> *"I daresay you haven't had much practice," said the Queen.*
> *"When I was your age, I always did it for half an hour a day.*
> *Why, sometimes I've believed as many as*
> *six impossible things before breakfast."*
>
> *- Lewis Carroll -*

*"Seeing is a rather curious thing for the
alternatives have always existed.
So if we were not able to see them, then
this is because they did not fit our logic
and our theory of what ought to exist."*

- Herbst -

Chapter 7

Reducing Just a Home Loan

*"One of the greatest disservices you can do a man
is to lend him money he cannot pay back."*

- Jessie H. Jones -

This chapter outlines in more detail how another couple - David and Sheryl - used the Mortgage Elimination™ System to reduce the term of their home loan from 20 years 4 months (making bi-weekly repayments) down to 9 years 11 months and will save $83,216 in interest. You will also see how the Mortgage Elimination™ System is far superior to the bi-weekly repayment program.

Case Study - David & Sheryl

PROFILE

LOAN AMOUNT:	$101,313.
INCOME:	$36,000 per year.
LOAN TERM:	Reduced from 20 years 4 months to 9 years 11 months.
INTEREST SAVINGS:	$83,216

Rather than having their income go into a checking account, David and Sheryl also took out a Home Equity Line of Credit and into which they are now directly putting all of their income. This has the immediate effect of reducing their home loan, and of course, interest is then calculated on the reduced outstanding daily balance.

The table on the next page illustrates how this couple's loan reduced from $101,313 to $96,941 over the first 12 month period. It shows their first year's monthly loan balances according to their Mortgage Elimination™ Plan.

As you can see, based on their current lifestyle, their Mortgage Elimination™ Plan showed them:

1. How much interest they would have to pay for their home loan at the end of each month; and

2. The amount they would owe on their home loan at the end of each month.

Cash Flow Forecast: David & Sheryl

	Jan	Feb	Mar	Apr	May	Jun	Jul	Aug	Sep	Oct	Nov	Dec
Opening Balance	101,313	100,980	100,387	99,866	99,143	98,659	97,926	97,833	97,268	97,493	97,281	96,756
Income:	2483	2483	2483	2483	2483	2483	2483	2483	2483	2483	2483	2483
Expenses												
Property Taxes	0	0	0	0	0	0	0	0	0	0	0	0
Water Rates	0	0	0	0	0	0	445	0	474	0	0	0
Electricity	70	0	70	0	70	0	70	0	70	0	70	0
Gas	0	72	0	0	72	0	0	72	0	0	72	0
Telephone	0	75	0	0	75	0	0	75	0	0	75	0
Home Maintenance	20	20	20	20	20	20	20	20	20	20	20	20
House Insurance	0	0	0	0	0	0	0	0	0	0	0	500
Food & Groceries	542	542	542	542	542	542	542	542	542	542	542	542
Clothing & Footwear	20	20	20	20	20	20	20	20	20	20	20	20
Newspapers/Magazines	13	13	13	13	13	13	13	13	13	13	13	13
Alcohol Tobacco	10	10	10	10	10	10	10	10	10	10	10	10
Health Insurance	50	50	50	50	50	50	50	50	50	50	50	50
Gifts	20	20	20	20	0	0	0	0	0	0	0	0
X-mas	0	0	0	0	0	0	0	0	0	0	400	400
Entertainment	20	20	20	20	20	20	20	20	20	20	20	20
Holidays	0	0	0	0	0	0	0	0	0	500	0	0
School Expenses	87	87	87	87	87	87	87	87	87	87	87	87
Accounting Fees	0	0	0	0	0	0	500	0	0	0	0	0
Miscellaneous	108	108	108	108	108	108	108	108	108	108	108	108
Vehicle 1 Insurance	0	0	0	0	0	0	0	0	418	0	0	0
Vehicle 1 Registration	258	0	0	0	0	0	0	0	0	0	0	0
Vehicle 1 Fuel/Oil	90	90	90	90	90	90	90	90	90	90	90	90
Vehicle 1 Service	0	0	0	100	0	0	0	0	0	0	0	0
INTEREST CHARGED	842	783	832	800	822	790	815	811	786	811	781	808
Closing Balance	100,980	100,387	99,866	99,143	98,659	97,926	97,833	97,268	97,493	97,281	96,756	96,941

As I mentioned earlier, HELOCs are *interest only* loans. So from now on, David & Sheryl are only required to make interest only payments on their loan, which will vary according to their daily balance. Furthermore, the principal on their home loan will now be reduced by withdrawing their budgeted living expenses, as per their Mortgage Elimination™ Plan, and leaving all surplus funds in their HELOC. The figures in their Mortgage Elimination™ Plan are extremely important because they act as guideposts as to how much they should pay off their loan at any given time. It's like having a *financial map* for their home loan. I will explain why this is so crucial in more detail in Part C, but right now I want you to focus on getting the workings of our Key Principle squarely ingrained in your mind.

The calculations for David and Sheryl's End of Month Loan Balances schedule were based on a HELOC interest rate of 9.9%, and according to their particular income and expenses, David & Sheryl's Mortgage Elimination™ Plan showed the following:

Home Equity Line of Credit	
End of Year	**Loan Balance**
1	$96,941
2	$91,722
3	$85,327
4	$77,769
5	$68,902
6	$58,565
7	$46,577
8	$32,738
9	$16,826
10	$0

As you can see, their plan showed that if they maintained their current lifestyle, they would completely Own Their Home in the tenth year.

Comparing the differences

To get an exact idea of how much time and interest they could save, David & Sheryl compared the results of using the Mortgage Elimination™ Way with their original P&I loan results.

P&I Home Loan: $101,313
Interest Rate: 9.9%
Repayments: $445 bi-weekly

Comparison of Original P&I Loan with Mortgage Elimination™ Way		
After Year	Loan Balance (Original P&I)	Loan Balance (HELOC)
1	$99,671	$96,941
2	$97,866	$91,722
3	$95,870	$85,327
4	$93,667	$77,769
5	$91,236	$68,902
6	$88,553	$58,565
7	$85,593	$46,577
8	$82,325	$32,738
9	$78,719	$16,826
10	$74,739	$0
11	$70,347	$0
12	$65,499	$0
13	$60,150	$0
14	$54,246	$0
15	$47,730	$0
16	$40,539	$0
17	$32,603	$0
18	$23,845	$0
19	$14,180	$0
20	$3,512	$0
21	$0	$0

David & Sheryl's Mortgage Elimination™ Plan showed that if they maintained their current lifestyle and used the Mortgage Elimination™ System, they would completely pay off their home loan by the end of the 10th year (9 years 11 months to be exact).

This loan would have taken them 20 years and 4 months to pay out using their original P&I loan (paid bi-weekly), and by the end of the 10th year, they would still have owed $74,739 of the principal - *plus interest!*

In effect, David & Sheryl reduced their home loan term from 20 years 4 months down to 9 years 11 months with an interest saving of $83,216.

What about future expenses?

One of the great features of a HELOC is that it allows you to withdraw funds back up to the original limit of the loan at any time, without you having to spend hundreds of dollars on refinancing. David and Sheryl loved this feature because they were planning to spend $10,000 on renovating their home in February of the 5th year of their loan.

However, they also realized that now, every time they withdrew money they hadn't accounted for, it would affect the term of their loan and the amount of interest they would eventually pay. Therefore, they wanted to make an informed decision as to whether it was worth spending this money and increasing the term of their loan. To help them arrive at this decision, they used my software program to do another set of calculations based on withdrawing $10,000 in February of the fifth year from their HELOC.

The analysis showed that with the $10,000 expense in year five of the loan, it would increase the term from 9 years 11 months to 10 years 11 months. This meant they could now make an informed decision as to whether this expense was worth extending their home loan for another 12 months.

 HOT TIP

If you are wondering where you can get the 'right tools' to help you calculate these types of scenarios, I'll tell you more about them in Part C - 'Making It Work For You.'

"It's lack of faith that makes people afraid of meeting challenges, and I believe in myself."

- Muhammad Ali -

Summary

You can see that there's nothing mysterious about accelerating the reduction of a home loan using my Mortgage Elimination™ System. Basically, David & Sheryl took the following steps to drastically reduce the term of their home loan:

1. They empowered themselves with knowledge so, they knew exactly what to do, how to do it, and made sure they had the right mindset to take charge of their home loan in order to pay it off years sooner.

2. They refinanced to the type of loan (HELOC) required to make this concept work.

3. They created a personalized Mortgage Elimination™ Plan, which allowed them to make a comparison with their old P&I loan and the Mortgage Elimination™ Way. It also enabled them to see how much time and interest they would save by switching over to this new repayment method, as well as giving them guideposts in terms of what monthly balances to aim for with their HELOC.

4. They continue to take control of their finances and make informed decisions by examining the impact that spending their money will have on the term of their new home loan.

 HOT TIP

In Part C, I will explain in more detail exactly what steps you need to take in order to Own Your Home Years Sooner.

"I learned that if you want to make it bad enough,
no matter how bad it is, you can make it."

- Gale Sayers -

Chapter 8
Reducing a Home and Personal Loan

"Enthusiasm is the greatest asset in the world.
It beats money and power and influence."

- Henry Chester -

In this chapter we will look at Simon and Fiona - a professional working couple with no children.

As you will see, this couple had a slightly different financial position than the couple from the previous chapter, in that they had a Home Loan, a Personal Loan, as well as some savings.

By utilizing my Mortgage Elimination™ System and a Home Equity Line of Credit (HELOC), Simon and Fiona reduced their total loan of $191,000 from 13 years 2 months, down to 5 years 11 months, with an interest saving of $84,847.

Case Study - Simon & Fiona

PROFILE
HOME LOAN: $174,270 @ 9.75%
PERSONAL LOAN: $12,000 @ 14%
PERSONAL SAVINGS: $5,000 @ 3%

To start with, Simon and Fiona consolidated their personal loan of $12,000 at 14% interest with their HELOC, which was available at 9.9%, because it represented an interest saving of 4.1% on the personal loan (i.e., 14% - 9.9% = 4.1%). Straight away this translated into a dollar saving of $492 in the first year.

Furthermore, this couple had $5,000 in a personal savings account earning 3% interest, which they transferred into their HELOC once it was set up. This meant they now saved interest at the rate of 9.9% on $5,000 of their HELOC – remember saving interest is the same as earning interest – and by doing this, Simon and Fiona now received a *threefold return on their savings*. What's more, this money was still available to them at call. In terms of a dollar amount, they saved an additional $345 a year in interest on their home loan – *tax free!*

HOT TIP

If you have high interest bearing loans, then it may be a good idea for you to try and consolidate them with your HELOC. If you have money in a savings account, then deposit that money into your HELOC because in most cases, the interest you save will be a lot more than the interest you are earning.

How much will the bank lend them?

When borrowing money, one of the first things lenders always look at is the amount of the loan you need in relation to the value of your property. This is called the Loan to Valuation ratio, or 'LTV'.

The value of Simon and Fiona's property was $250,000, and their total refinancing costs added up to $4,760. Instead of paying for these refinancing costs with up front cash, they chose to consolidate these costs with their new loan instead. This meant that their total loan amount increased to $191,000. In Part C, I will show you how to calculate your LTV to qualify for the type of HELOC required to make this system work – and how not to pay an application fee!

The spectacular results

As you will see, even though this couple's refinancing costs added up to $4,760, they were still able to pay off all of their debts in 5 years 11 months and save $84,847 in interest – not a bad return on $4,760, wouldn't you say?

Remember that the way they arrived at a loan amount of $191,000 was by consolidating their personal loan ($12,000) and refinancing costs ($4,760) with their original P&I home loan of $174,240.

Once Simon and Fiona created their Mortgage Elimination™ Plan, it gave them the results on the next page. Please note that I have duplicated only a summary of their first year Cash Flow Forecast results for illustration purposes.

As you can see from the results of their Mortgage Elimination™ Plan, it shows Simon and Fiona's total debt/loan being reduced from $191,000 to $166,927 over the first 12 months using the Mortgage Elimination™ System.

Summary of Cash Flow and End of Month Loan Balances (Year 1)				
	April	*May*	*June*	*July*
Opening Balance	191,000	183,736	181,743	179,444
Minus Income	10,301	5,301	5,301	5,301
Plus Expenses	1,554	1,793	1,554	2,729
Plus Interest	1,483	1,515	1,448	1,487
Closing Balance	183,736	181,743	179,444	178,359
	August	*September*	*October*	*November*
Opening Balance	178,359	176,241	174,927	172,619
Minus Income	5,301	5,301	5,301	5,301
Plus Expenses	1,714	2,575	1,554	4,793
Plus Interest	1,469	1,412	1,439	1,400
Closing Balance	176,241	174,927	172,619	173,511
	December	*January*	*February*	*March*
Opening Balance	173,511	172,401	170,661	168,803
Minus Income	5,301	5,301	5,301	5,301
Plus Expenses	2,754	2,138	2,126	2,033
Plus Interest	1,437	1,423	1,317	1,392
Closing Balance	172,401	170,661	168,803	166,927

Simon and Fiona's Yearly Loan Balances were as follows (remember, their loan calculations were based on an interest rate of 9.9%):

Home Equity Line of Credit (HELOC)	
End of Year	**Loan Balance**
1	$166,927
2	$142,079
3	$112,997
4	$79,569
5	$41,299
6	$0

The calculations showed that if Simon and Fiona maintained their lifestyle and current living expenses as outlined in their Mortgage Elimination™ Plan, they would completely pay off *all* of their debts in 5 years 11 months.

Comparing the differences

Simon and Fiona wanted to compare their new repayment proposal with their original P&I loan. So, they used my specialized software program to create a Mortgage Elimination™ Plan that gave them the following results:

Comparison of Original P&I Loan with Mortgage Elimination™ Way		
After Year	Original P&I (9.75%)	HELOC (9.9%)
0	$174,000	$191,000
1	$167,514	$166,927
2	$160,068	$142,079
3	$151,864	$112,997
4	$142,822	$79,569
5	$132,859	$41,299
6	$121,879	$0

They saw that by maintaining their current lifestyle and using the Mortgage Elimination™ System, their home loan *and* their personal loan would be totally paid out by the end of the 6th year. Had they stayed with their original P&I Loan repayment method, they would still have owed $121,879 at the end of the 6th year, and taken another 7 years and 2 months to pay out their home loan.

In effect, this couple will reduce their loan term from over 13 years down to 5 years 11 months with an interest saving of $84,847. As you can imagine, they were jumping for joy knowing that they would save this amount of interest on their home loan.

INSIDER SECRET

This couple actually went from an interest rate of 9.75% on their original P&I Loan up to 9.9% with a HELOC, and they will *still* pay off all of their loans faster than their original repayment method! This seems to defy all logic because, as I said earlier, most people focus purely on the interest rate when choosing a loan.

However, as you now know, it is the way interest is calculated and charged, and how you make your repayments, which makes all the difference. The reason for this is that by having all of your funds sitting in your home loan for as long as possible, you will make every cent you earn work harder for you. And even though you may have to pay setup costs and refinance to a higher interest rate, this repayment method could still cut years off of your home loan. Here's an exaggerated example to illustrate this point.

Imagine if you had a $50,000 HELOC at 20% interest, but had $48,000 sitting in it. This means that you are only paying interest on $2,000, and not on the full $50,000. In other words, you only pay interest on the money you use, and there are a myriad of ways as to how you can keep that balance down – more on this in Chapter 17 'Saving Even More Interest'.

> *" 'Lucky' people are simply those who think continually about what they want and then attract it into their lives."*
>
> *- Brian Tracy -*

Summary

You can see that reducing the term of a home loan is simply a matter of understanding how the interest on your home loan is calculated, charged, and then taking advantage of these facts.

Furthermore, even though you may have to pay fees to refinance to a Home Equity Line of Credit and move to a higher interest rate than your current P&I loan, you could still cut years off of your home loan. That's because this repayment method allows you to make the most efficient use of your existing financial resources by allowing your money to sit in your home loan until you use it. This of course can save you a substantial amount of interest.

 HOT TIP

Even though I said that in order to qualify for a HELOC you must have at least 10% equity in your home and pay for refinancing costs, at the time of writing this edition, I was working with several lenders to relax these criteria. For the latest update, please go to my website, click on 'What to do' and select 'Step 2 - Get the Right Loan'. Then click on 'Review Lenders' where you can see which lenders have joined my 'Lender Affiliate Program', their loan to value ratios, as well as my assessment of the advantages and disadvantages of their loan products.

In the next chapter, I will share with you the different options you can enact in order to apply my Mortgage Elimination™ System.

"They are able because they think they are able."

- Virgil -

Chapter 9
Options for Consideration

"Two roads diverged in a wood,
and I - I took the one less traveled by,
and that has made all the difference."

- Robert Frost -

In this chapter I am going to outline how to apply my Mortgage Elimination™ System, no matter which country you reside in. However, I am going to concentrate the introduction on the American banking and mortgage industries because they are rather unique (international readers please refer to Chapter 19 for more options). Let me begin by sharing with you a . . .

Brief history

Prior to 1980, American banks and savings and loan associations (S&Ls) lent their own money to borrowers, usually at fixed rates between 6-7%. Then in the late 1970s, rate restrictions on the banking industry were lifted, and soon after that, inflation rose to 14%. This led to short-term interest rates going even higher, with the prime rate reaching as high as a staggering 23%.

You didn't have to be a rocket scientist to see that anyone lending out money at a fixed rate of 6% and having to pay 14% to a depositor who supported the loan was not going to stay in business for very long. In fact, a lot of lenders who had been around for some time did go under, merged, or were taken over and liquidated for this very reason.

As a result, lenders and regulators alike acknowledged that an alternative had to be found for lending out volatile short-term funds, and the Variable Rate Mortgages (VRM) or Adjustable Rate Mortgages (ARM) were born. These types of loans essentially lock in a lender's profit margin at a specific rate, let's say 2%. That is, if the lender pays their depositors 4% then they will lend you that money at 6%. If they pay depositors 6.5% then they will lend you that money at 8.5%, and so on.

Taking this approach, regulators ensured that 'Portfolio Lenders' (institutions lending against their depositor's funds and keeping the loans 'in house') would not endanger themselves by going under amidst a volatile interest rate environment.

Rise of the secondary market

The problem that arose as a result of the VRMs and ARMs was that borrowers still wanted long term fixed rate loans, but the lenders, who were mostly portfolio lenders, did not want to offer them anymore. Consequently, this demand for fixed rate loans gave rise to what is now called the 'Secondary Mortgage Market'.

What happened is that quasi-governmental companies such as the Federal National Mortgage Association (FNMA), commonly known as 'Fannie Mae' and the Federal Home Loan Mortgage Corporation (FHLMC), called 'Freddie Mac', stepped in to fill the void left by the portfolio lenders. These companies buy fixed rate mortgages from banks, S&Ls, and mortgage bankers. They then package them into 'pools' that might total $10 or $20 million, and then sell interest in the pools to institutional investors such as pension plans and mutual funds.

There is a lot more to this story, but for our purposes, it's sufficient to say that this is the way the secondary market provides liquidity to the primary lending market. It is the means by which your local bank, S&L, or mortgage banker can offer long term fixed rate loans that it originates.

Consequently, you will find that soon after you take out your home loan, you will be mailing your mortgage payment to a company other than the one that originated your loan. That's because in 95% of cases, mortgage companies no longer lend you their own money. They simply package loans that they can then sell to some other company immediately or at some time in the near future.

What does this have to do with you?

One of the things you must realize is that the interest rate of a HELOC (or any Revolving Line of Credit type of loan) is ALWAYS tied to the variable interest rate because in most cases, only portfolio lenders originate these types of loans.

Again, because lenders secure the loans against their depositor's funds, they have to ensure that they retain a profit margin in order to protect themselves from any potential rises in interest rates. Therefore, you can expect the interest rate of your HELOC to fluctuate during the time you have it. The only exception is that some lenders may fix the interest rate for a short period of time in order to win your business, and then the loan will revert to whatever the variable rate happens to be after the fixed rate term has expired.

Your choices are . . .

After reading the chapters in this part of the book, you might think that in order to Own Your Home Years Sooner, you have to change your entire loan to a Home Equity Line of Credit (HELOC) and then apply the principle of Mortgage Elimination™ I have been talking about. I deliberately structured the book this way so as not to go into the intricacies of the options you can exercise too soon. That's because I wanted you to focus on getting the workings of the Key Principle down pat first. Now that I believe you have a good handle on that concept, I can tell you that in actual fact, you have three options you can exercise to apply my Mortgage Elimination™ System - all of which have their own pros and cons. These options are:

1. Transfer your entire P&I loan to a HELOC;

2. Take out a smaller HELOC as a second mortgage (recommended);

3. Take out a personal Revolving Line of Credit (RLOC).

Notice that no matter which option you choose to exercise, you will have to take out a Revolving Line of Credit type of loan. That's because at present, most banking systems only offer this type of loan product to make my Mortgage Elimination™ System operable (UK, New Zealand, and Australian readers, please refer to Chapter 19 for more options).

Having said that, I am working on getting lenders to introduce other loan options in the US. So, if you are a lender reading this and are interested in working with my team and me to develop alternative and better loan products for the American market, please use the 'Contact Us' option through my website for more details. You can also refer to Appendix 2 for a general outline of our 'Lender Affiliate' program. For the rest of you folks wanting to be updated on what's happening, I invite you to log on to my website on a regular basis. Alternatively, you can subscribe to my FREE online newsletter so that my team and I can send you updates on this issue, as well as other news and hot tips to help you Own Your Home Years Sooner.

Let's now examine each of the three options I just mentioned.

OPTION 1 · Convert your entire P&I Loan to a HELOC

This option is like the situations I have described in Chapters 6 through 8. With this approach, you refinance your entire P&I loan to a HELOC and then apply my Mortgage Elimination™ System to reduce it quicker.

Once your HELOC is set up this way, all of your income is paid directly into your HELOC, as well as any savings are transferred into it. This has the immediate effect of reducing your loan by the amount of income that goes into it, thus decreasing the amount of interest you are charged. You then treat your HELOC as a day-to-day transaction account, whereby you withdraw your budgeted expenses in accordance with your Mortgage Elimination™ Plan, via an ATM Card and checkbook as required, and leave the rest of your funds in the HELOC.

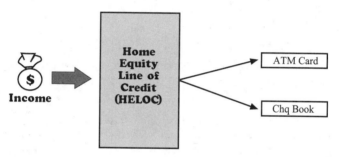

If you choose to apply Option 1, here are the advantages and disadvantages of this approach:

Advantages:

• Easy to manage because you only have one account to deal with.

• You have access to a larger 'pool' of funds if needed. For example, if you decide to access the equity in your home for a large expense item, such as upgrading your car or renovations, you can withdraw that money without having to refinance to increase the limit of your HELOC. That's if you have built up the necessary equity to do this.

Disadvantages:

- You are exposing your entire loan amount to the variable interest rate.

- If you don't have a plan, the right tools, and the willingness to manage this type of loan properly, you will never pay it off because you can keep drawing the funds right up to the original approved loan amount at any time.

- Depending on which lender you go with, the refinancing costs can be significant – yet avoidable.

OPTION 2 - Take out a smaller HELOC as a second mortgage (recommended)

I would recommend that you give this option serious consideration because it has some major advantages over Option 1. That is, rather than taking out a HELOC for the entire loan amount of your mortgage, you would take out a smaller HELOC as a second mortgage and then apply the Mortgage Elimination™ System to reduce it quicker.

Let's take a look at how this can be set up to work using an example.

Case Study - Brian & Eva

PROFILE
HOME LOAN (P&I):	$150,000
INTEREST RATE:	Fixed @ 5.75%
MONTHLY PAYMENT:	$875.36
LOAN TERM:	30 years
APPRAISED VALUE OF HOME:	$250,000

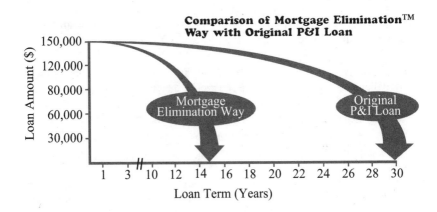

Comparison of Mortgage Elimination™ Way with Original P&I Loan

Brian and Eva had a $150,000 P&I loan, which they had secured a fixed interest rate for 30 years at 5.75%, and they were making monthly repayments of $875.36 toward it.

They worked out that if they took out the entire loan amount as a HELOC and applied the Mortgage Elimination™ System, they could Own Their Home in less than half the time and save $104,347 in interest.

However, they did not want to give up the security of the fixed interest rate, but still wanted to apply the Mortgage Elimination™ System to reduce their home loan quicker.

The great news is that if you are in a similar predicament, there is a workable solution that gives you the best of both worlds. That is, you can take out a smaller HELOC as a second mortgage, to which you apply the Mortgage Elimination™ System, while leaving the larger portion of your loan at the fixed rate as a P&I loan. The best part is that you can still achieve exactly the same results as Option 1 by doing this. The other advantage is that your refinancing costs will not be as high, or nil, when compared to refinancing your entire loan amount.

The following is what Brian and Eva did. I know it may look confusing at first, but it's not. Just follow the diagrams and the explanations, and reread this section several times if you have to because this is most likely what you will choose to do also.

Step 1: They empowered themselves with knowledge and made a commitment to make the Mortgage Elimination™ System work in their lives.

Step 2: They made sure they could, and refinanced to the right type of loan that allowed them to apply the Mortgage Elimination™ System.

Step 3: They created a personalized Mortgage Elimination™ Plan, which showed them exactly how much time and money they would save by subscribing to the Mortgage Elimination™ Way - compared to their original P&I loan repayment method – without significantly changing their lifestyle. Furthermore, they now use this plan as a financial map to stay on track to ensure that they will pay out their mortgage in the projected time.

Brian and Eva worked out that they had enough equity in their home to take out a $75,000 HELOC as a second mortgage (I'll show you how to work that out in part C). However, they didn't want or need to access this entire amount of money, so they only took out a HELOC for $10,000 - also available to them at 5.75% (see diagram below).

<table>
<tr><td>

$10,000 HELOC
available @
5.75% variable
interest rate

No interest is
charged until
the funds are
drawn down

</td><td>

$150,000
P&I Loan

Fixed
@ 5.75%

</td></tr>
</table>

They then wrote a check from their HELOC for $5,000 and made a lump sum deposit into their P&I loan that brought it down to $145,000. Therefore, only the portion of the HELOC that is drawn down is charged interest. The reason they did not lump sum the entire $10,000 into their P&I loan was because they wanted to have a 'safety-buffer-fund' in case of emergencies (see diagram below).

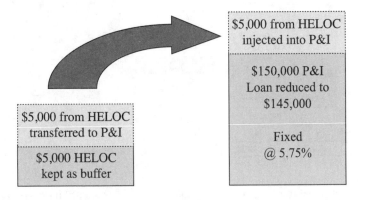

At this stage, the immediate ramifications of this action are obvious. That is, if you made a lump sum payment of $5,000 into your P&I loan, of course you would reduce the loan term and save interest – assuming you kept making the same repayments. For example, in Brian and Eva's case, when they injected $5,000 as a lump sum into their P&I loan and kept making their $875.36 monthly repayment toward it, it had the effect of reducing their P&I loan by 2 years 5 months, and saved them $21,067 in interest.

"But wait, all you've done is transfer the debt, and you're expecting me to believe that this is going to save me all that time and interest?" I hear you ask.

"Ahh, outstanding question", I say, and here's more of the story.

Yes, they did transfer $5,000 of debt from their original P&I loan into a HELOC.

However, they could now take full advantage of the Key Principle by depositing all of their income into their HELOC, thereby reducing the amount of interest they were charged. This was something they were not able to do had they stayed with their original P&I loan.

The outcome was that they are now depositing all of their income into their HELOC and only withdrawing money as they need it, according to their Mortgage Elimination™ Plan. They are also maintaining their $875.36 monthly repayment toward their P&I loan from the HELOC (see diagram below):

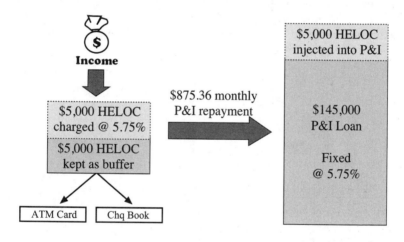

In effect, what they are doing is focusing all of their attention on paying off the $5,000 HELOC as fast as they can by using the Mortgage Elimination™ Way, without significantly changing their lifestyle. When they have reduced the $5,000 balance of the HELOC down to $0, they will make another lump sum payment into their P&I loan from the HELOC and start the whole process over again.

This will of course reduce the P&I loan by another $5,000, and by maintaining the $875.36 monthly repayment toward it, it will again significantly reduce the P&I loan term accordingly. Remember Brian and Eva are now gaining a two-fold advantage with their hard earned money:

1. They are accelerating the reduction of their P&I loan every time they make a lump sum payment into it from their HELOC; and,

2. They are saving interest on the HELOC because they are taking full advantage of our Key Principle to reduce the amount of interest they are charged.

They will keep repeating this process until both loans are completely paid off.

Having said that, now that Brian and Eva have a Mortgage Elimination™ Plan - which they never did before - they are much more aware of their personal finances. One of the things they realized was that they actually have surplus funds left over at the end of each month that they used to spend, but now, they choose to leave this money in the HELOC, thereby reducing the debt even quicker. The reason they do this is because they now have the right tool to see the effect of leaving these funds in their loan compared to spending them. Ultimately, I have found that this is what happens when people start becoming more conscious of their finances and start making informed decisions about how to spend their hard earned money.

Is it really worth it?

The next thing you may think is that the amount of interest savings are so small on the HELOC that it hardly seems like a worthwhile exercise. Well, let's just have another look at the daily interest charged for Martin & Genevieve's loan for the first four months (case example from Chapter 4).

Month	Daily Balance	Daily Interest Charged
Jan	$100,000.00	$27.40
Feb	$99,940.70	$27.38
Mar	$99,798.64	$27.34
Apr	$99,737.48	$27.32

As you can see, there is only a difference of two cents a day between the amount of daily interest charged the first and the second month, and only four cents a day for the next two months. Friends, it is these itty-bitty cents that add up over the years and amount to tens, if not hundreds of thousands of lost dollars paid out in interest to your lender. And, what my Mortgage Elimination™

System does is to make sure that these humble pennies stay in your pocket, so that you are not at the mercy of compound interest.

Consequently, by taking charge of their home loan, Brian and Eva are now deciding how long it will take them to pay it off, and they are well on their way to Owning Their Home Years Sooner – without making extra interest payments.

Overview

Let me take you through a summary of what Brian and Eva did. Once again, don't worry too much because when it comes time for you to do this, I've made sure you have detailed instructions every step of the way. At this stage I just want to give you an overview.

✓ Brian and Eva decided that they had the right mindset to make the Mortgage Elimination™ System work in their lives to Own Their Home Years Sooner.

✓ They made sure they could and then refinanced to the right loan that allowed them to apply the Mortgage Elimination™ System in their lives. To that end, they applied for and were approved for a $10,000 HELOC.

✓ They created a personalized Mortgage Elimination™ Plan that showed them exactly how much time and money they would save by subscribing to the Mortgage Elimination™ Way compared to their P&I loan repayment method – without significantly changing their lifestyle.

✓ Once they got the loan, they injected $5,000 from their HELOC into their $150,000 P&I loan, thereby reducing its balance to $145,000.

✓ By continuing to make $875.36 monthly repayment toward their P&I loan from the HELOC (after injecting $5,000 into it) it reduced the P&I loan term by 2 years 5 months and will save them $21,067 in interest.

✓ They are now depositing ALL of their income into their HELOC and only withdrawing money as they need it, in accordance with their Mortgage Elimination™ Plan.

✓ Once they pay off their HELOC, they will make another lump sum deposit of $5,000 from it into their P&I loan.

✓ They will keep repeating this cycle until all loans are completely paid off, which in their case will result in a time saving of over 15 years and $104,347 in interest.

Advantages:

- Extremely easy to setup because you are not refinancing the entire P&I loan amount.

- Loan setup costs are very low, or in some cases may be nil.

- You are exposing only a small amount of your total home loan debt to the variable interest rate.

- Depending on the size of your P&I loan, the HELOC interest rate can be significantly higher and your 'average interest rate' would still be closer to the P&I loan interest rate. For example, in Brian and Eva's case, if their HELOC had been at 10% instead of 5.75%, the average interest rate for the two loans would still only be 5.89%. That's because only the smaller of the two loans is exposed to the higher interest rate in the early years.

- You can use the HELOC exactly as described to pay off any debt, especially high interest bearing ones, before applying it to reduce your home loan.

- If you find this concept is not working for you, you can always go back to your original P&I repayment method without having to incur exorbitant refinancing costs.

- From a psychological point of view, the smaller HELOC amount will seem like a manageable sized loan that you will see being eliminated very quickly, right before your eyes, which in turn will give you more motivation to achieve the forecasted term in your Mortgage Elimination™ Plan.

Disadvantages:

- Again, if you don't have a plan, the right tools, and the willingness to manage this type of loan properly, you will never pay it off because you can keep drawing the funds right up to the original approved loan amount at any time. However, this will be for a much smaller amount, and you are still required to make payments toward your P&I loan.

- If you have a big expense item you want to spend money on in the future, you will either have to refinance your HELOC, or, make sure you have a large enough 'buffer fund' to accommodate the expense. For example, if you only take out a HELOC for $5,000 and you want to spend $10,000 on home renovations in year 4, then you will have to ensure that you have enough 'reserves' in the HELOC to accommodate this planned future expense.

OPTION 3 - Take out a Personal Revolving Line of Credit (RLOC)

If you find that you can't qualify for a HELOC because your Loan to Valuation ratio exceeds what a lender is agreeable to, or for some other reason, then you may want to take out a personal Revolving Line of Credit (RLOC).

With this option, you would do exactly the same thing as explained in Option 2. The biggest drawback to this is that because this type of loan is most likely not secured against your property, the interest rate will be higher. How much higher will depend on the lender you decide to apply for your loan with, and other factors, such as your credit history. Other than that, all of the other advantages and disadvantages are the same as Option 2.

Having said this, my personal recommendation is that you DO NOT exercise this option, but rather work on building the equity in your home so you can qualify for a HELOC (refer to Chapter 17 for more details on ways you can do this).

"You don't have to be great to get started,
but you have to get started to be great."

- Les Brown -

Part C

Making it Work for You

*"What you think will direct what you say,
what you say will direct what you do,
what you do will direct your Destiny."*

- Suze Orman -

Now, in order to actually apply my Mortgage Elimination™ System, there are only two more steps you need to take. And these are:

Step 2 – Get The Right Loan*
Step 3 – Create Your Plan*

In effect, these last steps will help you to acquire the tools to actually apply my Mortgage Elimination™ System in your life, so you can Own Your Home Years Sooner.

So if you're ready, let's do it.

*__International readers__: please note that steps 2 & 3 as outlined on this page are in reverse order for you. For more information and explanation, please refer to Chapter 19.

The Mortgage Elimination™ System Revisited

Do you recall in the introduction to Part B when I said:

*"To Own Your Home Years Sooner, YOU DON'T have to be
a financial genius, or have tons of money?"*

Well, I want you to know that I'm going to keep my word on this.

First of all, I want to point out that I have never set myself up as an 'expert' who is indispensable, and to whom you need to pay thousands of dollars to. My whole intent is to empower you to take charge of your home loan to pay it off sooner.

Now that you have read Part B, let me say that you're doing great because you've made it through the toughest part of the book. I also hope you realize that we are not dealing with rocket science here. I'm just an ordinary guy who discovered a way to help you take advantage of a very basic principle that will help you pay less interest on your home loan. And all I've done is break down that information into understandable, actionable steps, and have systemized the entire process. So from now on, if you wish to join the tens of thousands of people who are Owning Their Homes Years Sooner – without making extra interest payments - it's a simple case of following the instructions in this part of the book.

So if you're ready, we are going to get down to the nitty gritty. Now I don't know about you, but I've had enough of books and seminars that tell you 'what' to do, but fall way short on showing you 'how' to do it.

Well, that's where I part company from the mainstream because I believe in laying everything out on the table – up front – and making sure people get value for their money. My promise to you is that you don't have to pay $3,000 to a consultant to show you how to Own Your Home Years Sooner - because for $24.95, the price of this book – I'm going to show you how to do that yourself.

In the next couple of chapters I'm not only going to walk you through the steps to apply my Mortgage Elimination™ System in your life, but I will also show you where to get the tools and resources to make that happen. For example, you now know that you will need to take out a HELOC to make this concept work. So, on my website you will not only find lenders who have joined my 'Lender Affiliate' program, but they have also agreed to charge you a nil application fee for a HELOC (in most cases). They are also willing to pay for your 12 month subscription fee, so you can use my online software program to create your personalized Mortgage Elimination™ Plan. As you will see, this final step is vitally important to help you stay on track with your goal of accelerated home ownership. And, I have negotiated for you to access this software program at no charge for the first 12 months, saving you an additional $200 for the first year (see Chapter 14 for more details).

Moreover, if you are a lender reading this book and wish to be a part of my 'Lender Affiliate' program, for the benefit of my readers, all you have to do is contact my team through my website (also refer to Appendix 2).

Before we move on to the first 'how-to' chapter, I want you to ask yourself this very important question: Do you have . . .

The right stuff to make this system work for you

The reason I ask this is because I can give you all of the knowledge and tools in the world, but unless you have set and made the decision to achieve your goal of accelerated home ownership, none of this is going to be of any use to you.

Let me share with you two examples of what I mean.

Julie (not her real name) is an intelligent, motivated, professional, with a well paying job. She asked me to help her with rearranging her finances because she was crumbling under the weight of a hefty mortgage, as well as credit card debts totaling nearly $35,000 – which seemed to be growing every month.

We started by consolidating her high interest bearing credit card debts (some were at 18%), and had her take out a second mortgage on the house as a P&I loan, with a much lower interest rate than the credit cards. This was a precaution to see how she would do and if she was willing to change her out of control spending habits. In addition to this, she had what most would consider an extravagant hobby of keeping and riding horses (she owned two of them), and they cost her thousands of dollars each year - everything from vet bills to board and lodging for these animals.

Julie asked me to go along with her to see the loan officer. I still remember sitting in the waiting room with her as she was practically shaking with fear and shame for getting herself into this predicament. That was in 1998. I tried to help her as much as I could, but by 2002, Julie still had the two mortgages, both horses, and her credit cards were maxed out again. Don't get me wrong, I'm not saying to give up your life and live like a hermit. I just want to encourage you to make wise choices with your money.

In contrast, here is an e-mail I received from someone I have never met, but who decided to take self-responsibility to improve her life, as well as her family's, simply by following the steps in this book. Please note: Some of the comments in parentheses have been added by me to clarify the point.

Dear Mr. Gill,

I thought that I would jot down a few lines for you about our new life.

Our life prior to your book was a wasteful one. My husband and I have two good incomes and two children. We have had a mortgage (various ones) over the last ten years and have done nothing with them. We had a full $5,000 credit card and a personal car loan of about $5,000.

We lived from paycheck to paycheck and still managed to owe the taxation office thousands of dollars each year, which would take months to pay off. We worked out one year that we had spent about $7,000 on fast food alone, as well as spending $130+ each week on groceries.

We had not been able to afford a decent holiday, and I had not had more than 10 days off in the last 12 years.

Our combined income is about $80,000+, and I own my own business, which of course was in the red and had been for the last 4 years, by about $7,000.

In Feb/March of this year, a friend of my husband's (who both work in the real estate industry) showed us a little red book and told us to read it. Within 2 weeks we had both read the book and talked about it with everyone, so we decided to talk to our bank, the XYZ (name withheld by the author to protect the guilty).

Man, they suck.

They said they would consider our application, but after asking them the questions you have in the book, I decided that this was not a good thing. We went to the ABC bank, and they sounded pretty good. We put in a submission, and it took them over 6 weeks to get back to us with a NO. I was angry, because I knew that I had wasted not only time, but also money in the form of interest. I actually had to bail up the bank manager in the shopping center to get him to give me an answer.

To cut a long story short, we finally found a bank that was willing to give us the loan, and after getting the house evaluations done, had our approval in 24 hours. I was amazed. We also got a new credit card with only a $3,000 limit, so we could make it work straight away - like you recommend (see Chapter 17 on how to do this to save more interest).

We have no bank fees for deposits or withdrawals, etc (I'm sure you know about them). But the best thing is, we use your program on the website to keep track of where we are now and where we are going. It is so true that you must have a PLAN. I panicked when I couldn't get on your (Australian) website for a while, thinking "please Harj, don't stop!" But we managed to resolve that.

Anyway, since April of this year, we have done the following:

a. Paid off our $5,000 credit card
b. Paid off our $5,000 personal car loan
c. Saved $8,000
d. Pay off our credit card every month - in full like you recommend
e. My business is in the black to the tune of $6,000
f. Got back pay from one of my part time employers of $10,000 (I was so motivated to find money, that I checked my pay slips)
g. We are going on our first big holiday in 29 sleeps for 4 weeks in Queensland - Australia, paid in full - with empty credit cards awaiting us, and still money left in the bank.

All going well, I will be expanding my business with extra staff coming on board early next year, and plan to make the business work for us as a tool, not a liability. Meanwhile, our mortgage (which was $130,000 when we started) will be over and done with in four and half years.

I have now passed your website address (no one is getting my book!) on to lots of people, and I am getting the same stories from them. Thanks to you, our lives have changed completely. My stress levels are much lower, our marriage is better, and we have our priorities straight.

Thanks again Mr. Gill.

DARRALYN D.

Northern Territory - Australia

The people I have just described and in the case studies I refer to throughout this book all had dreams that they thought would take years to fulfill, mainly because of the mortgage hanging over their heads. However, ALL of those who made the decision to overcome this obstacle are now enjoying the lifestyle they had envisioned for themselves.

I have found through years of consulting experience that the one thing every single person or couple who have Owned Their Home Years Sooner has in common is a willingness to take charge of their lives – especially in the area of personal finance. And to back up my observations, I once again quote Drs. Thomas Stanley and William Danko from their excellent book, *The Millionaire Next Door*. These gentlemen have carried out one of the most comprehensive studies into the habits and mindsets of the financially free amongst us, and one of the things they found is that . . .

> " . . . *these millionaires are frugal, persistent and well educated, although they don't always score high on their SAT tests. They are not workaholics, but finishers: they always complete their tasks or projects. They exercise frequently and are disciplined.*"

Now, doesn't that just about summarize the attributes you need to succeed in any endeavor in life?

The point I want to make in this introduction is that I'm a nuts and bolts kind of guy. I know for a fact that my Mortgage Elimination™ System works, as long as you have the willingness to take charge of your home loan. Having said that, I also understand that there are as many different reasons as to why one person does something and another doesn't - as there are stars in the sky. So if you think there is an issue you need to address about your money habits before you commence this program, then I would highly recommend the following resources as a starting point.

Books: *The Courage to Be Rich*   (Suze Orman)
               The Science of Getting Rich (Wallace D. Wattles)
Seminars: The Millionaire Mind   (T. Harv Eker)
               The Science of Getting Rich (available as an online study course)

If you want to know more information about where to get these resources, please go to my website, click on 'Toolbox', and refer to the section on "Wealth Education and Empowerment."

For the rest of you, let's get cracking.

> "*The moment of enlightenment is when a person's dreams of possibilities become images of probabilities.*"
>
> - Vic Braden -

Chapter 10
Get the Right Loan (Step 2)

*"The indispensable first step to getting the things
you want out of life is this: Decide what you want."*

- Ben Stein -

In the next few chapters, I am going to help you complete Step 2 by first describing a Home Equity Line of Credit (HELOC) in more detail, as well as the features you should look for in a 'good' HELOC to apply with my Mortgage Elimination™ System. Also included is a checklist of questions to ask a lender, should you choose to do the legwork yourself. Furthermore, I am going to recommend and assume that you are going to exercise Option 2 from Chapter 9 by taking out a 'small' HELOC as a second mortgage.

The reason that this is Step 2 in my system is because if you can't qualify for this type of loan, for whatever reason, then I don't want you to go to Step 3 (Create Your Plan) and pay the subscription fee to use my online software program. As I mentioned earlier, my company has an 'Affiliate Program' with lenders who are willing to pay this fee on your behalf, as well as to waive their loan application fee for their HELOCs (in most cases). In other words, I don't want you to spend any more money than the price of this book when my team and I have already arranged for you to get these critical tools at no charge.

In case you're wondering if I am playing favorites with the lenders, let me assure you that I'm not. My 'Affiliate Program' is open to any lender that meets my criteria. As you have probably gathered by the e-mail from Darralyn D. in the introduction to Part C, she met with a lot of resistance from lenders before she actually found one who approved her loan. That is precisely the reason I put this 'Affiliate Program' into place. I know from first hand experience what you are going to face if you approach a lender who is not conversant with this revolutionary system of Mortgage Elimination™ at this early introductory stage in this country. I can tell you that you are going to meet a lot of blank faces, silly replies to your informed questions, and sometimes even downright contempt for what you are attempting to do. That's because you will be challenging long held institutional paradigms that have never been questioned, and it will take about four years for the banking industry to catch up with what you now know.

To illustrate my point, let me share with you another story.

When this book and system were reviewed in their original form on a national current affairs program in Australia (February 10th, 1997), it immediately became a best seller. We sold thousands of copies in the first week and people rushed to their banks in droves asking for a HELOC in accordance with the characteristics I describe. Sadly, most were met with staunch skepticism and disbelief from the lending staff themselves, and were told that such a system could not possibly work and that it was a scam. Well, we sold over 150,000 copies of my books in that country, and it caused nothing short of a banking revolution over there. So much so that now, every lender offers the type of loan product I recommend to use in one form or another in the Australian editions of my book. Furthermore, in all of that time, I only had one customer ever ask for their money back, and that was in 1997 - when this system was first introduced. I was so taken aback that I kept the handwritten letter for all of these years. Below is a scanned copy of the letter explaining why this customer wanted a refund, and because it may be difficult to read, I have transcribed the entire text on the next page.

NOTE: I have added the information in parentheses and bold for clarification and emphasis.

Dear Sir,

I first viewed your segment on "The Kerry-Anne Kennely Show" (national TV talk show in Australia) and was excited by the chance to own my home years sooner through your promoted scheme.

I phoned the number on the show and was assured that our bank 'Commonwealth' (second largest bank in Australia) was and would be prepared to negotiate a similar scheme of repayments for me.

Since receiving your booklet and other information leaflets, I phoned 'The Commonwealth' and was informed that **they would not be part of any such scheme.**

Today 2-6-97 (2nd June, 1997) I phoned your freecall helpline xxxx xxx xxx (Australia only) explained my dilemma to your consultant and was advised to return the book to receive a full refund. This I have done.

Would you please credit my Master Card No xxxx xxxx xxxx with $39.95 as promised

Yours faithfully,

Mrs. C.E. Tranent

The irony of all this is that five years later (2002), the bank in question started heavily promoting a loan product that they developed in accordance with my criteria for a 'good' HELOC, and they use the language from my book to do so. Have a look at the copy of the bank's ad on the next two pages and read the wording. I'm sure you'll see some similarities. So much for "not wanting to be a part of any such scheme!"

Anyway, I hope you can now see why I set up the 'Lender Affiliate' program. It is in place so you can save a lot of legwork in finding the best HELOCs for use with my Mortgage Elimination™ System. If you would like to know more about the exact nature of the relationship between American Mortgage Eliminators™, LLC and the Affiliate Lenders, please refer to Appendix 6.

Commonwealth Bank advertisement in
The Sunday Times on July 14th, 2002

See enlargement of text on next page

Enlargement of text from previous page

1. Compared to a standard home loan a Viridian Line of Credit Home Loan is a flexible, all-in-one account that builds equity faster by reducing your loan balance, twenty-four hours a day, seven days a week.

2. By depositing your salary and savings into Viridian you automatically reduce your loan balance and the amount of daily interest owing.

3. Having your Commonwealth Bank Credit Card linked to Viridian means you can use your credit card to make your day-to-day purchases. Each month your entire credit card balance can be swept to your Viridian account. This lets you take advantage of the 'up to 55 days interest-free period' on your credit card, saving you even more in interest costs.

4. Viridian also lets you use the equity built up in your home to fund other investments (like property, shares or managed funds) at home loan rates.

5. Plus, you have the choice of competitive interest rate options.

Make it happen.

Chapter 11
What to Look for in a 'Good' HELOC

*"It's a funny thing about life; if you refuse to accept
anything but the best, you very often get it."*

- W. Somerset Maugham -

Outlined in this chapter are the general features of a HELOC and what you
should look for in the type to successfully apply with my Mortgage Elimi-
nation™ System. The topics we are going to cover are:

1. Set Up Costs
2. Interest Rate Charges and Features
3. Borrowing Limit
4. Loan Term
5. Borrowing Terms and Conditions
6. Payment Terms and Conditions

Before we discuss these, let me give you a . . .

 HOT TIP

There is a distinct and significant difference between a **Home Equity
Line of Credit** (HELOC) and a **Home Equity Loan** (HEL) - so
please, don't make the mistake of applying for the wrong type of loan.
The reason you could easily confuse the two is because Home Equity
Loans are usually heavily advertised in the media, whereas HELOCs
are relatively obscure at this stage. The only similarity between these
loans is that both a Home Equity Loan and a HELOC are secured by
the equity in your home. However, a Home Equity Loan is in most
cases a P&I loan because it has a fixed repayment schedule and term.

A HELOC, on the other hand, works like any other revolving line of
credit because it allows you to write checks or make credit card
purchases and withdrawals against the equity in your home on an
ongoing basis. Therefore, it is a HELOC that you need and NOT a
Home Equity Loan. Furthermore, you will need a HELOC with very
specific features as described in this chapter to successfully apply with
my Mortgage Elimination™ System.

1. Set Up Costs

Some lenders may charge hundreds of dollars to set up a HELOC. These fees may include the following: a loan application fee; property appraisal fee; up-front charges, such as one or more points; and other closing costs, such as fees for attorneys, title search, mortgage preparation and filing, property and title insurance, and taxes.

Ideal: *$0 application fee*
No up-front charges in the form of points
$0 closing costs

2. Interest Rate Charges and Features

As I said earlier, HELOCs normally come with a variable interest rate unless the lender offers an unusually low fixed-introductory rate (usually for the first 6 months). Federal regulations require that lenders base their variable rate on a publicly available index, such as the prime rate published in some major daily newspapers, or a U.S. Treasury bill rate. Therefore, you can expect your HELOC interest rate to change as it mirrors fluctuations in the index. Also remember that every lender will add a margin to the index rate, and because of this, it is important to be aware of what that added margin is, as different lenders add different margins.

Another federal requirement is that variable rate loans secured by a dwelling must have a 'Ceiling' (or 'Cap') on how much your interest rate may increase over the life of the loan. Some variable rate loans may limit how much your payment may increase, as well as how low your interest rate may fall if interest rates drop.

Due to the above, your loan agreement will most likely include clauses that permit the lender to reduce your Credit Limit, and/or not allow you to draw additional funds during any period that the interest rate reaches the 'Cap'. It is important to be aware that the smaller the difference between the Cap rate and the variable rate at the time you were approved for the loan, the more likely you will encounter these terms and conditions being activated in the event of fluctuations in the prime rate.

Ideal: *The main thing you want here is to ensure that the lender's margin is not exorbitant (i.e., not too far above the prime rate) and what their 'Cap' rate is*

3. Borrowing Limit

To determine the borrowing limit, all lenders will examine your income, your debts, your ability to repay, your credit history, as well as other financial obligations. To determine the actual amount you can borrow (in the case of a HELOC, called a 'Credit Limit'), lenders take a percentage of the appraised value of your home and subtract the balance owed on the existing mortgage(s). This gives them a ratio of debt in relation to the value of the property - called the Loan to Valuation ratio (LTV). Depending on which lender you apply for your loan with, and the type of loan you apply for, they may go as high as 120% LTV. The downside to this is that the higher your LTV is above 80%, the more you may have to pay, both in terms of setup costs, as well as higher interest rates. However, most lenders will only go up to 90% LTV for a HELOC.

Here is a quick example of calculating the LTV. Let's say that the appraised value of your home is $200,000, your mortgage is $100,000, and the lender will go as high as 90% LTV. The amount you could borrow would be:

Appraised value of home	=	$200,000
Lender LTV	=	90%
% of appraised value	=	$180,000 (i.e., 90% x $200,000)
Minus mortgage debt	=	-$100,000
Potential 'Credit Limit'	=	$80,000

Ideal: *High LTV (90%), but no penalties in terms of having to pay higher application fees, closing costs (preferably $0), or higher interest rates if your LTV is above 80%*

4. Loan Term

Lenders often set a fixed time during which you can borrow money, usually around 10 years for a HELOC. When this time period is over, the lender may allow you to renew your HELOC. If not, then you will not be allowed to borrow additional funds once the time has expired, and you may have to pay any outstanding balance in full as a balloon payment. Others may permit you to repay the outstanding balance over a fixed period by converting your HELOC into a P&I loan for a set number of years – usually 10 years.

Ideal: *Ability to renew HELOC at end of contractual period at no charge*

5. Borrowing Terms and Conditions

Once your HELOC is approved, you may be able to borrow up to your 'Credit Limit' whenever you want – typically using a checkbook, and in some cases a VISA Debit Card as well. However, some lenders may place limitations on how you can use their HELOC. For example, you may be required to withdraw/borrow a minimum amount each time ($300), and/or keep a minimum amount outstanding, and/or be required to take out an initial advance when you first get your HELOC. Some lenders may also impose an annual membership or maintenance fee and charge you a transaction fee every time you drawdown funds from your HELOC.

Ideal: *No annual membership or maintenance fees*
Unlimited withdrawals/draw-downs via checkbook and/or VISA Debit
ATM card attached to the HELOC
No per transaction fees and/or charges
No limit on the size of withdrawals/draw-downs
Not required to take out initial advance when you first get your loan

6. Payment Terms and Conditions

Some lenders may impose a minimum payment that covers a portion of the principal plus the interest. However in most cases, the principal portion will not be enough to repay the HELOC by the end of the loan term. Other lenders may allow interest only payments during the life of the loan, and either require you to make a balloon payment, renew the loan, or turn it into a P&I loan with a set term at the end of the loan period.

Given that your goal is not to be in debt forever, but to use your HELOC as a tool in association with the Mortgage Elimination™ System, you want one that allows you to pay interest only, make payments as often as you like - without restrictions on the amount paid into the loan.

Ideally, for ease of management, you want a HELOC that allows you to directly deposit your income into the HELOC and have the lender withdraw the interest from it, so you don't have to juggle separate accounts, or write monthly checks to make the interest payments. Finally, you want a HELOC with no early payout fees.

Ideal: *Can make interest-only payments*
Unlimited deposits/payments
No limit on the size of deposits/payments

Income/salary can be paid directly into the HELOC
Monthly interest automatically deducted from the HELOC
No early payout fees

The next chapter helps you work out how much you can borrow and gives some pointers on how much to borrow before you start approaching any lenders. It also contains a checklist of what you should look for in a 'good' HELOC in accordance with the features I have just outlined. By the way, if you want to do all of the legwork yourself, you may want to make a photocopy of the checklist and use it to assess the HELOCs of different lenders by asking the questions on it. It is important that you do this because many lenders offer a HELOC, but not all of them have the features necessary to successfully apply with my Mortgage Elimination™ System.

 HOT TIP

If you want to save yourself a lot of time, hassle, and money in finding the best HELOC to apply with my Mortgage Elimination™ System, you may want to check out my website. There you will find lenders whom my team and I have identified as having a 'good' HELOC in accordance with the characteristics I just outlined.

What's more, in most cases, these 'Affiliate Lenders' have also agreed to charge a $0 application fee and pay your 12 month subscription fee to access my online Mortgage Elimination™ Plan Software program - saving you an additional $200 for the first year. You will see just how important this tool is in helping you Own Your Home Years Sooner in Chapter 14.

"The highest use of capital is not to make more money,
but to make money do more for the betterment of life."

- Henry Ford -

Chapter 12
Calculate How Much You Can Borrow

"In the book of life, the answers are not in the back!"

- Charlie Brown -

As I said in the introduction, in this step (2), I am going to recommend and assume that you are going to exercise Option 2 from Chapter 9 by taking out a 'small' HELOC as a second mortgage to apply my Mortgage Elimination™ System with.

Remember, to determine the actual amount you can borrow (in the case of a HELOC, called a 'Credit Limit'), lenders take a percentage of the appraised value of your home and subtract the balance owed on the existing mortgage(s). This gives them a ratio of your overall debt in relation to the value of your property - called the Loan to Valuation ratio (LTV). Most lenders will go up to 90% LTV on a HELOC as a second mortgage. So let's work out how much you can borrow. To do this you will need to know your:

Appraised value of home   =   \$_____   = (A)

Current mortgage amount   =   \$_____   = (B)

Now take (A) x 90% = \$_____ = (C)

Next take (C) - (B)   = \$_____ (this is your potential credit or borrowing limit for a HELOC - based on a 90% LTV).

Keep in mind that you don't have to take out a HELOC for the entire amount of your approved credit limit. A \$10,000 limit will be adequate, so you can inject a lump sum of, say, \$5,000 into your P&I loan and have another \$5,000 as an 'emergency buffer'. Even having a \$5,000 HELOC will do the trick because the idea is to keep making periodic lump sum injections into your P&I loan as soon as you have built up that money in your HELOC. In the meantime, you will be gaining all of the interest benefits by taking full advantage of our Key Principle.

Now before I give you the checklist, what if the LTV of your current mortgage(s) is already above 90% and you don't qualify for a HELOC? Sadly, you are going to have trouble getting a HELOC because most lenders do not go above 90% LTV for this type of loan. Therefore, you can either wait until you build up enough equity to qualify, or take action now. By the way, you may want to also check my website for updates on lenders that have relaxed this criteria - since the last printing of this book.

A story of hope and persistence

Now before you get disheartened and upset, thinking that you wasted your money on this book, let's go back to basics.

I'm sure you realize by now that what I have been proposing all along is NOT a quick fix solution. My system requires you to take charge of not only your home loan, but also your financial lifestyle if you are truly serious about Owning Your Home Years Sooner.

Let me give you an example to illustrate what I mean.

In my earlier consulting days, a young couple, Phil and Tina, came to see me and couldn't wait to get started with my Mortgage Elimination™ System. I soon found out that their great enthusiasm was the result of talking with friends for whom I had already consulted and set up the program for. And all of these friends were doing nothing more than simply achieving the forecasted results in their Mortgage Elimination™ Plan – which, by the way, is quite impressive to someone not familiar with what is possible.

When I did the calculations for Phil and Tina, the results showed that they could own their home in less than half of the time projected for their P&I loan and would save over $70,000 in interest. You can only imagine how elated they were to hear this and couldn't wait to tell all of their friends that they, too, would be joining them on the fast track to home ownership.

What's more, I could see by their motivation that Phil and Tina would be real Trojans once they got started and would not only meet their projected goal of accelerated home ownership, but would most likely Own Their Home a lot sooner than the time forecast in their Mortgage Elimination™ Plan.

The only glitch was that they simply did not have enough equity in their home to get a HELOC to start the program at that time. What was even more depressing for them was that we calculated that according to their current loan repayments and the size of their mortgage, it would take them at least another three years before they could qualify for this type of loan.

You don't have to be a psychic to know that by the end of our session, they started to feel extremely frustrated and victimized. That is when I reminded them that "life is a series of choices, and it's up to each of us to make wise choices." So, we spent the next hour discussing some of the things they could do to build the equity in their home to bring down their LTV, so that they could qualify for a HELOC and get started with my system.

In summary, here's what they did:

- They took a good look at their spending habits, created a budget and cut down on some items that were not essential, such as getting take-out three nights a week, having cable TV, etc. I know that this last item is an essential for some people - akin to removing oxygen from the atmosphere, but these are some of the choices you may have to make. In Phil and Tina's case, they used this 'surplus' money to make extra payments toward their P&I loan to bring down its balance, thus increasing the equity in their home.

- Next, they had several garage sales to get rid of the clutter in their home, and they also used this extra cash to inject into their P&I loan.

- They improved the value of their property by thousands of dollars by doing some landscaping. This proved to be the most profitable return on their time and investment. Not only did they build equity in their home in record time, but it also kept Phil and Tina focused and working together as a couple toward a common goal, thus improving their personal relationship in the process.

- Finally, they 'borrowed' some money from their parents, with a clear plan to pay it back, which they also injected into their P&I loan (see Chapter 17 for more details on how they did this).

The great news is that this couple came back to see me eight months later and are living proof of the old adage that 'necessity is the mother of all invention'. By doing all of the things we had discussed to build equity in their home, they not only qualified for a HELOC in record time and started my program, but the financial management skills they learned have now put them well on the road to Owning Their Home Years Sooner.

So, if you are in a similar predicament as Phil and Tina were, I can understand that it is frustrating. And I don't mean to preach here, but you too, have a choice. You can either sit around stewing and moping, or you can use that e-motion (energy-in-motion) by channeling it into constructive action. Be glad that you now know a better way to pay off your mortgage, and then, simply do what Phil and Tina did – take action. I guarantee that if you have half of the zeal they did, it won't take you long to get started with this system as well.

On the next page is the checklist I promised for a 'good' HELOC.

American Mortgage Eliminators™
Checklist of What to Look for in a 'Good' HELOC

Lender Name:_____

As far as using this checklist is concerned, you want to aim for having as many responses being the same as the option next to the question. And remember, don't be surprised if you get a lot of blank expressions, silly replies to your informed questions, or treated as if you have two heads when you begin your search for the perfect HELOC. Alternatively, to save yourself a lot of time, effort, and money, you can use my website to find a suitable lender.

* Do you charge an application fee for your HELOC? **No**
* Do you charge up-front fees in the form of points? **No**
* Are there any additional closing costs? **No**
* Do you have a short (48 hours) approval time? **Yes**
* How far is your margin above the prime rate? _____%
* What is your cap rate for the HELOC? _____%
* What is your maximum LTV? _____% **(ideal = 90% or above)**
* Are there penalties in terms of having to pay higher application fees, closing costs, or higher interest rates if my LTV is above 80%? **No**
* Is there a minimum amount I have to borrow? **No**
* If yes, what is that minimum amount? $_____
* Can I make interest-only payments? **Yes**
* Are there annual membership or maintenance fees? **No**
* Can I make withdrawals via ATM Debit Card and checkbook? **Yes**
* Can I make an unlimited number of withdrawals/draw-downs? **Yes**
* Is there a limit on the size of withdrawals/draw-downs? **No**
* Are there per transaction fees and/or charges? **No**
* Am I required to take out an initial advance (draw-down) when I first get my HELOC? **No**
* Can I make unlimited deposits/payments into the HELOC? **Yes**
* Is there a limit on the size of deposits/payments I can make? **No**
* Can I have my income/salary paid directly into the HELOC? **Yes**
* Can I have my monthly interest charges automatically deducted from the HELOC? **Yes**
* What is the period of the loan? _____ years.
* Are there early payout fees on this HELOC? **No**
* Can I renew my HELOC at the end of the contractual period at no charge? **Yes**

Chapter 13
Loan Application Procedures

"Tomorrow is the most important thing in life.
It comes unto us at midnight very clean. It's perfect when
it arrives and it puts itself in our hands. It hopes we've
learned something from yesterday."

- John Wayne -

Depending on how you apply for your HELOC (i.e., in person at a local branch or online), your application may take several minutes or several days to be approved. Having said that, all of our 'Affiliate Lenders' have their online application forms linked through my website, and most can give you a decision within minutes of submitting your application to them. Personally, I like this approach because it is not only fast, but also very convenient.

Furthermore, by submitting your HELOC application through my website, not only will you pay a $0 application fee (in most cases), but you can easily choose to have the lender pay for your 12 month subscription to use my online Mortgage Elimination™ Plan Software program – saving you $200 for the first 12 months. Remember that I have negotiated for you to receive these benefits, so you don't have to spend all that time and money searching for the best loan. Also, in most cases the option to have the lender pay for your 12 month membership fee is clearly displayed on the lender's online application form, as long as it is linked from my website. Otherwise, if you were to apply through a physical branch office of a lender, you may not be able to exercise this option because the loans officer may not be aware of our 'Lender Affiliate Program' and/or have access to the appropriate software-request-webpage through their branch computer system.

Applying online through my website (SAVE $200)

If you choose this option and wish to pay a $0 application fee (in most cases) and have the lender pay for your first 12 month subscription to use my online software program ($200 value), here's what to do:

1. Go to my website at www.MortgageFreeUSA.com and click on the menu item 'What to do', and select – 'Step 2 - Get The Right Loan'.

2. Once on this page, select 'Review Affiliate Lenders' – and review their loan(s).

3. Next, select the lender with a loan that best meets your needs, and click 'Begin Now'.

4. You will then see an "Important Instructions Page", which will tell you what to expect in terms of the loan application procedure and more importantly, how to get your FREE access to my online software program. Please read the information on this page, check the box that says, "YES - please send me the 'Software Request Authorization Form'. . ." Fill in the short details, and click "Apply Now."

5. This will take you to the lender's website to complete the loan application process, and you will know in a matter of minutes if your loan has been approved. Once that happens, in most cases you will also receive a set of physical loan documents by mail from the lender. These documents will outline the terms and conditions for the loan, and you will have to sign and return them to the lender to complete the loan approval process. Meanwhile, as part of Step 4 (above) my team will have already sent you the 'Software Request Authorization Form' - which you must complete and submit with your loan documents when you mail them to the lender. This is a necessary precaution to safeguard your privacy, and it also allows us to know where to send the login and password for you to access my online software program.

Upon settlement of your loan

Once the lender has received and verified your loan documents, you will be informed that the account is ready for operation. Checkbooks and ATM cards will be issued for your HELOC and mailed to you. As soon as we receive your details from the lender - as per the 'Software Request Authorization Form' - for verification, along with payment for the software subscription fee, my team will send you a complete set of instructions with a login and password to access my online Mortgage Elimination™ Plan Software program for 12 months - saving you $200.

Once you have all of these 'tools', your next and final step is to create your personalized Mortgage Elimination™ Plan, so that you can begin your new journey to Own Your Home Years Sooner - without making extra interest payments!

"You cannot build a reputation on what you intend to do."

- Liz Smith -

Chapter 14
Create Your Plan (Step 3)

*"Would you tell me please, which way I ought
to go from here?", asked Alice.
"That depends a great deal on where you
want to get to", said the Cat.
"I don't much care where', replied Alice.
"Then it doesn't matter which way you go," said the Cat.
" . . . so long as I get somewhere", added Alice.
"Oh you're sure to do that", said the Cat, "if you
only walk long enough."*

- Lewis Carroll -

You're doing great!

Welcome to the third and final step to apply my system by putting together your own personalized Mortgage Elimination™ Plan. I bet you're excited knowing that you, too, will soon be on your way to fulfilling your dream of Owning Your Home Years Sooner.

In that case, I better get you started and get out of the way!

To complete this step you will need your login and password to access my online Mortgage Elimination™ Plan Software program – unless you've decided to use a 'consultant'.

Please note: If you applied for your loan through one of the 'Affiliate Lenders' on my website, your loan has settled, and payment has been made to us by your lender for your 12 month software subscription fee, then the login and password has already been e-mailed to you by my team.

On the other hand, if your loan has settled and you have NOT RECEIVED this information, please contact my team through the 'Contact Us' form on my website, and we can verify if your lender has indeed paid this fee on your behalf.

Now before you take off and start inputting your data into the software program, let me take a moment to explain why your plan and having the right tool to create and manage it is so vitally important. That is if you seriously want to Own Your Home Years Sooner.

Planning is the key

In order for us to achieve any goal in Life, we must first plan for it.

Planning is simply a choice we make to create a desirable future for ourselves and the communities in which we live. We also have a choice not to do that because as William James once said:

> *"When you have to make a choice and don't make it, then that in itself is a choice."*

At certain breakpoints in our lives, just like the character, Alice, in Lewis Carroll's story, we too ask, "Which way ought I to go from here?"

The wise answer to that of course is, "It depends on where we want to get to."

Once we have decided on a destination or a goal, and we want to maximize our chances of getting there, we must prepare for the journey through the act of planning.

Simply put, planning is all about designing and bringing about a desired future that otherwise would not exist without our intervention. It is about deciding **what to do** and **how to do it** before action is required.

The value of goal setting and planning

Most of us have come to loathe the term planning and 'goal setting' because it reminds us too much of all the New Year's Eve resolutions that went unfulfilled. This is unfortunate because such continual disappointment has led many people to shy away from creating their lives according to their dreams. I must point out that this is not entirely our fault because we have never been given the proper framework for or tools with which to clearly plan, and systematically achieve a goal. I don't know about you, but I certainly was not taught this in school.

Well, all that is about to change because I am going to share with you one of the most potent SECRETS I have discovered to plan for and systematically achieve ANY goal in life – from losing weight to climbing Mt. Everest. And IF YOU FOLLOW THIS RECIPE EXACTLY, it is an absolutely FOOLPROOF formula for success. In fact, if you have children, I would highly recommend that you pass on this knowledge to them because it will help them throughout their lives. What's more, you can use your Mortgage Elimination™ Plan as a practical example of how it is done.

So what is this SECRET, FOOLPROOF recipe?

Well, I call the method I am about to share with you the 'SMART Way™' to set and achieve goals. The acronym S.M.A.R.T. stands for:

Specific
Measurable
Achievable
Results with a
Timeframe

How does this work, and why is it so effective?

To answer the above question, let me clarify what I mean by goals and plans and then explain the components in more detail.

GOALS: The aspirations we want to achieve, or a destination we want to reach.

A PLAN: The map or set of guidelines that gets us there.

Having said this, let me elaborate on the ingredients that a 'good' plan must have in order to succeed.

Specific: The first ingredient that is necessary in order to create a successful plan is that your goal has to be specific. If you don't know exactly what you want, then how can you even begin to take the steps to acquire it?

Measurable: The second ingredient necessary is that your plan has to have a tangible unit of measure such as time, money, weight, etc. This is extremely important because the unit of measure you use is directly tied to how you get feedback on your progress toward your goal.

Achievable: Next, in order to succeed with your plan, you must have a goal that is achievable. Otherwise you will never take your plan seriously enough to carry it through. For example, there's no point in saying you want to Own Your Home in the next six months when you know for a fact that this is not going to be possible – unless you come across an unexpected windfall.

Results with a **Timeframe**: These are two of the most critical ingredients a plan must have. That's because without knowing the results you are supposed to achieve within certain timeframes, how are you going to know whether you are making any progress toward your goal - and more importantly - be able to implement the measures necessary to get back on track if you are not?

Why you need a Mortgage Elimination™ Plan

I am sure you will have noticed by now that with a P&I loan, you didn't have to concern yourself with much other than writing a check to your lender for the repayments each month. Besides that, there was nothing else you had to do except make sure you have a job for the next 30 years to keep making those repayments.

In contrast, even though a HELOC is the best type of loan to apply my Mortgage Elimination™ System with, it does require some planning and diligence on your part. However, as you have seen, the rewards are well worth it.

Like I said earlier, a HELOC acts as a day-to-day transaction account, and you can redraw funds right up to the original credit limit. Therefore, the most important aspect to successfully use it to pay off your home or investment loan quicker is to manage it properly. That is, you have to have a plan and the right tool to effectively keep track of money going in and coming out of your HELOC. That's because from now on, every dollar you deposit and every dollar you withdraw from your new loan will have a direct impact on how long it takes you to Own Your Home. Please note that I cannot emphasize enough the importance of what I just said in this paragraph, and I do hope you follow through with my recommendation by creating and managing a Mortgage Elimination™ Plan for yourself once you get your HELOC.

Where can you get a plan?

Below are the two main options available to you in order to acquire a Mortgage Elimination™ Plan, what you can expect to pay, and the features of each option:

Hire a consultant:	$3,000	
Use my online software*†:	US$20	30 day subscription
	US$125	6 month subscription
	US$200	12 month subscription

* The prices quoted here were at the time of publication and may be subject to change. My team and I also have Special Offers from time to time. Furthermore, if you applied for your HELOC through one of the 'Affiliate Lenders' listed on my website, then you can expect for them to pay for your 12 month subscription to use this software program ($200 value). Please visit my website for more information and the latest updates.

† <u>International Readers</u>: Please refer to Chapter 19 for more information about a suggested course of action for your country of residence.

Hire a Consultant - $3,000: If you are thinking of hiring a consultant to create a plan for you, then you can expect to pay anywhere up to $3,000 for that privilege. What's more, don't expect for them to do anything more for you than what you can do for yourself by applying the information in this book and using the tools on my website.

If you are thinking of going down this path, then let me caution you with an Insider Secret . . .

 INSIDER SECRET

The situation I am about to describe sounds nefarious, but it has happened, and I don't want it to happen to you.

There have been so called mortgage reduction consultants who have not only charged a fee for their services, but also recommended/coerced customers into refinancing their entire P&I loan, so that they could pick up more money in the form of refinance commissions.

As you have seen, you don't need to refinance your entire P&I loan to make my system work because you only need a small HELOC to do so. This is especially the case if you have already taken advantage of the low interest rates that were available in the first half of 2003 by fixing the interest rate for your P&I loan.

Therefore, if a 'consultant' talks you into refinancing your entire loan, please make sure there are very legitimate reasons for you doing so. Otherwise you may be up for thousands of extra dollars in refinancing costs that you do not need to pay - in addition to your consultant's fee - because as you have seen, if you plan properly, you can set up this entire system for next to no cost.

Use my online software program: This is by far the most powerful and cost effective option you will ever come across to create your Mortgage Elimination™ Plan. This program has taken me over 8 years to develop and refine. It is the most sophisticated, yet user-friendly software program you will ever come across to apply my system. Please note that at the time of printing, I was also getting the software program verified by a certified actuary.

The best part is that you can access this program for a lot less than the $3,000 you can expect to pay a consultant!

 HOT TIP

If you applied for your HELOC through any one of the 'Affiliate Lenders' listed on my website, they will pay for your first 12 month's subscription ($200 value) to use this software program upon settlement of your loan. The reason the lenders are doing this is because they not only realize the importance of you having the right tool to manage and pay off your HELOC, but they want you as a long-term client as well.

What's in it for them is that if they help you Own Your Home Years Sooner, you may come back to them for your future loans and recommend others to do the same.

Furthermore, unbeknownst to you, you will have elevated yourself to what is known in certain circles as a 'blue-chip' client. That's because you will have demonstrated that you are astute and capable enough to handle money and are responsible enough to pay it back in record time. Consequently, all lenders want more people like you because they are not ogres, but business people who just happen to be in the business of lending money.

For full details on how to get a lender to sponsor your 12 month software subscription ($200 value), please refer to Chapter 13 for more details.

You have all the ingredients for SUCCESS

A little earlier I outlined all of the ingredients that must be present in order for you to successfully achieve a goal. Let me take a moment now to examine those components in relation to the Mortgage Elimination™ Plan you can create by using the online software program on my website.

Specific: One of the main reasons that tens of thousands of people have been so successful in paying off their home loans years sooner by using my software program is because it allows them to create an extremely accurate Mortgage Elimination™ Plan. This plan takes into account your income and living expenses and then calculates for you exactly how much of your loan you should pay off at the end of each month and each year, as well as the total amount of time it will take for you to completely Own Your Home. Now you can't get any more specific than that!

Let me mention just three of the many features that make this software program so accurate and unique.

i. **You Can Segment Your Income Into 'Blocks':** For example, at present you may have a double income coming in, but there may be a period where you only have one income for a certain amount of time. My online software program gives you the flexibility to cater to such changes by allowing you to specify the period of time for the double income, the period where you are only expecting one income, and then a return to having a double income once again.

ii. **You Can Update Your Plan with 'ACTUAL' Figures:** My program allows you to input your 'Actual' loan balances as shown on your monthly loan statements. It then automatically updates the remaining figures in your Mortgage Elimination™ Plan to reflect this latest data.

iii. **Uses 'Real Time' Income & Expenses:** Believe it or not, I have seen a few charlatan companies and consultants out there that take your income and expenses for an entire year and then 'average' these figures to give you your monthly cashflow forecast. This will lead to extreme inaccuracies in your Mortgage Elimination™ Plan and has caused many people to mismanage their HELOCs. In contrast, my program uses your 'actual' income and expenses, as they occur, to maximize the accuracy, and help you stay on track with your plan.

Measurable: In terms of measurable attributes, my plan gives you two interrelated units of measure. One is dollars, and the other is time. These units of measure will leave no doubt in your mind as to the progress you can and are making toward Owning Your Home.

Achievable: In terms of achievability, my software program let's you know what is possible for you with *your* income, *your* expenses, and the size of *your* home loan. It also allows you to work out different scenarios to see which ones enable you to realistically Own Your Home Years Sooner.

Results With a **Timeframe**: Some people (especially bank staff and financial advisors) will tell you that you need an iron will and superhuman discipline to manage a HELOC properly. Well, let me share with you some facts that are backed up by tens of thousands of people who have already used my system to debunk this major misconception:

The Number 1 reason most people don't and cannot budget properly, or manage a HELOC, is because they don't have the right tools to do so.

I bet that like most people, whenever you spend your hard earned cash right now, you probably have no way of assessing how each income or expense affects your financial position in the future, especially in relation to paying off your home loan sooner.

I believe this simple fact alone accounts for why most people have never been able to budget, or if they have a budget, have not been able to stick to it.

In contrast, when using a HELOC in conjunction with my online Mortgage Elimination™ Plan Software program, you will see a direct relationship between the income you earn and the money you spend on the overall term of your home loan. The best part is that it allows you to dictate how soon you want to Own Your Home by allowing you to manipulate any number of variables.

For example, 'what if' you wanted to know the effect of:

1. Depositing/withdrawing lump sum amounts in a specific month and year (e.g., depositing tax refunds, paying for renovations, holidays, etc.)?

2. Increasing/decreasing your income by $x a week/month/quarter, etc.?

3. Increasing/decreasing the interest rate?

4. Increasing/decreasing any expenses by $y a week/bi-weekly/month, etc.?

By using my online software program, you will be able to accurately calculate the effect that each of these 'what if' scenarios will have on the overall term of your home loan. So from now on, every time you want to spend your money, you will be able to make informed decisions based on facts. You can then decide whether it would be better to spend your money now or wait until a more suitable time.

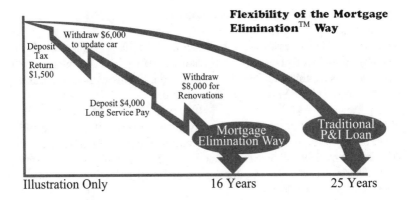

Flexibility of the Mortgage Elimination™ Way

Deposit Tax Return $1,500

Withdraw $6,000 to update car

Deposit $4,000 Long Service Pay

Withdraw $8,000 for Renovations

Mortgage Elimination Way

Traditional P&I Loan

Illustration Only   16 Years   25 Years

I have found from personal experience that the SECRET as to why every one of my readers who Owned Their Home Years Sooner (many exceeding their expectation) was because of this great tool.

Why?

Because it gives you instant feedback about the effect that your income and spending habits will have on the overall term of your home loan.

Now that you know all of the reasons to create and manage your Mortgage Elimination™ Plan, please go to my website, click on 'LOGIN', enter your login and password, and then click 'login'.

Once you enter the secure area of the website, simply follow the step-by-step instructions to create your plan.

> *"The best time to plant a tree is twenty years ago.*
> *The second best time to plant a tree is today."*
>
> *- African Proverb -*

Summary

The SECRET to successfully achieving any goal in life is to make certain that you have a SMART plan and that you stick to it. That is, your plan must be Specific, Measurable, Achievable and give you Results with a Timeframe. I call this the SMART Way™ to achieve a goal.

When I was consulting, I observed many people rushing off and refinancing to a HELOC without having a plan to pay it back. Six months later, they wondered why they still owed the bank the same amount of money they started with. This was especially true for those using a HELOC without a plan and the right tools to manage it.

This is not the fault of the bank, the loan, or my system. It is simply a case of people not willing to take responsibility to prepare themselves properly.

Therefore, my professional recommendation is: DO NOT DO ANYTHING UNLESS YOU ARE ALSO WILLING TO CREATE AND MANAGE YOUR OWN PERSONALIZED MORTGAGE ELIMINATION™ PLAN, and you have the correct tools to do this properly. The reason your Mortgage Elimination™ Plan is so critical is because it will act as your 'financial map' that will help you move closer to your destination of Owning Your Home Years Sooner.

If you follow this dictum, you will most certainly achieve your goal.

*"The world steps aside for those who
know where they are going."*

- Anon -

Chapter 15
Putting it all Together

"If you can't explain it to a six year old,
you don't understand it yourself."

- Albert Einstein -

Congratulations!

I'm assuming you've got your HELOC approved and settled, you've received your checkbooks and VISA Debit Cards from your lender, and you've put together your Mortgage Elimination™ Plan.

In this chapter, I'm going to guide you into tying up some loose ends to help you effectively manage and pay off your new loan as soon as possible.

Here's what to do

❏ Get yourself organized by acquiring a binder or a file where you will keep ALL of your loan documents, statements, bills, etc. – especially your Mortgage Elimination™ Plan – and put this file in a safe place. This is important because you are making a fresh start, and you want to approach your new journey of accelerated home ownership as if you are in total command. And, the best way to do that is to get yourself organized.

❏ Next, take the 'Projected Loan Term' sheet from your Mortgage Elimination™ Plan and stick it on the door of your refrigerator. Look at it every single day and say to yourself, "This is what I can and will do."

❏ Inform your employer to deposit your pay into your HELOC from now on – if you get paid electronically. At the same time, transfer all of your savings and any extra funds into your HELOC. Remember, you want to keep that loan balance as low as possible from now on.

If you are exercising Option 2 (from Chapter 9) by taking out a smaller HELOC as a second mortgage, then you will need to follow these additional steps:

❏ Write a check from your HELOC for the amount of lump sum you wish to inject into your P&I loan, ready to send off to your lender.

❏ Make sure you phone the lender of your P&I loan in advance and tell them that you will be making this extra payment amount along with your regular repayment. Ensure that the extra payment you will be making is used to immediately reduce your P&I loan principal and not used as an 'advance' for the following month's repayment.

☐ Give the lender of your P&I loan another call about a week after you have mailed your payment to make sure the above has happened.

☐ All you have to do now is focus your attention on your HELOC, and pay it off as fast as you can. As soon as you've done that, make another lump sum injection into your P&I loan from it, and keep repeating this process until all of your loans are paid off.

 HOT TIP

As soon as you get the monthly loan statement from your lender, look at the End of Month Closing Balance for the appropriate month from your Mortgage Elimination™ Plan and compare that with the balance on your loan statement. If the 'Projected' figure in your plan is the same as the 'Actual' figure as shown in your loan statement, that's fantastic. And if you keep achieving these monthly balances, YOU WILL pay off your loan within the projected time as shown in your Mortgage Elimination™ Plan.

However, if you ever happen to stray off track, just log back on to my website and input your latest data, and see where you can manipulate your spending the following month so you can bring yourself back on course. If you do this on a regular basis (monthly), you will find that it will very quickly turn into a habit – and this is one habit that is definitely worth developing.

I told you this wasn't rocket science!

"The secret of success is constancy of purpose."

- Benjamin Disraeli -

Chapter 16
Common Questions

*"If we did all the things we are capable of doing,
we would literally astound ourselves."*

- Thomas Edison -

In the final chapter of this section, I want to address some common questions that always arise. As you can see, I have grouped them into two major categories, and an updated list of FAQs is always available on my website.

General questions

1. Is American Mortgage Eliminators™ a licensed mortgage company?
2. I took advantage of the low interest rates recently and refinanced my existing home loan. Will your Mortgage Elimination™ System still be able to help me?
3. I have less than 10 years to pay on my existing home loan. Will your Mortgage Elimination™ System still benefit me?
4. I could repay my mortgage right now – why would I want to?
5. I have heard of 'consultants' doing a similar thing and charging $3,000 for it. Why do you charge so little?
6. If your Mortgage Elimination™ System is so good, why haven't I heard about it?
7. Don't the banks lose out with your system?
8. Do I have to change what I am doing – because I don't want to change?
9. I'm a first-time homebuyer. How do I go about applying your Mortgage Elimination™ System?

Specific loan and software questions

10. I already have a HELOC. Do I have to change to a new one?
11. What do I have to do to get the Free 12 month subscription to use your online Mortgage Elimination™ Plan Software program?
12. Can I still get the Free 12 month access to your software program if I already have a HELOC?
13. If I go through a broker to get my HELOC, can I still get the Free 12 months access to use your software program?
14. I already have a HELOC with one of the 'Affiliate Lenders' listed on your website. Can I still get the Free 12 months access to your software program?

15. I applied for my HELOC through your website with one of your 'Affiliate Lenders' listed there. My loan has been approved and settled. I have received my checkbooks and VISA Debit Cards, but I haven't received my login and password from you to access your online software program. What do I have to do to get these?
16. I can't get a loan because I have a bad credit rating. What can I do?

1. Is American Mortgage Eliminators™ a licensed mortgage company?

A. No. I do, however, consider my company to be a leader and educator in the field of Mortgage Elimination™ strategies.

2. I took advantage of the low interest rates recently and refinanced my existing home loan. Will your Mortgage Elimination™ System still be able to help me?

A. Absolutely. You did the right thing by refinancing to the lowest interest rate you could find. Now, I can show you how to Own Your Home Even Sooner because with my Mortgage Elimination™ System, you will always pay less money in the form of interest - despite what your interest rate is – and as you have read, this is the key to accelerated home ownership.

3. I have less than 10 years to pay on my existing home loan. Will your Mortgage Elimination™ System still benefit me?

A. First, congratulations on being in this wonderful position. Second, if you want to ensure a successful retirement, you should be considering investing in other cash or saleable assets. My system will not only help you Own Your Home Years Sooner, but will also help you own those assets years sooner, should you have to borrow money to acquire them. Please refer to Chapter 18 for further information.

4. I could repay my mortgage right now – why would I want to?

A. My Mortgage Elimination™ System is really a vehicle to help you build your asset base and create wealth. Financial experts say that we need at least $1.2 million dollars in cash or saleable assets by the time we retire. The only true way to accomplish this for most people is by borrowing money to purchase assets over time. My system simply reduces the cost of borrowing this money, so you build equity much faster than traditional loan repayment methods. As you have seen, my system is by no means a get-rich-quick scheme. It is a life-long strategy to accumulate cash or saleable assets. Please refer to Chapter 18 for further information.

5. I have heard of 'consultants' doing a similar thing and charging $3,000 for it. Why do you charge so little?

A. The only difference between you and these so-called 'consultants' charging exorbitant fees is that they have the knowledge to make this work and you didn't – until now! I believe in empowering ordinary people with the knowledge and tools rather than setting myself up as the only one capable of doing this for people. To that end, as you have seen, everything you need to understand to set up your own Mortgage Elimination™ Plan is explained in this book, and all of the tools you need with which to apply it are on my website.

6. If your Mortgage Elimination™ System is so good, why haven't I heard about it before?

A. I have only recently introduced the concept to this country. However, I have been educating people about this new way of loan repayment in Australia since 1997. In that time, my books and system have revolutionized the entire banking system of that country and helped tens of thousands of people to Own Their Homes Years Sooner. This accelerated mortgage reduction system has now become a part of the national psyche of that country – and I hope to achieve the same outcome here.

7. Don't the banks lose out with your system?

A. In the short term – yes, because their customers will Own Their Homes Years Sooner by using this system, therefore resulting in the lender making less money through interest. However, those lenders who take a long-term view, will soon realize that by actually creating loan products that allow customers to Own Their Homes Years Sooner, it will result in actual benefits for them in the long term. Consider that when the average family repays their 30 year mortgage in less than 10 years. What happens is that they will usually make a conscious decision to 'buy-up' again - often well before the 10 years. And each time they buy, they will usually refinance with the same lender - if the lender has serviced them well. Thus they will pay interest on the new loan. And each time they 'buy-up', they will build their asset base. Therefore, with my Mortgage Elimination™ System, both the lender and the borrower win!

8. Do I have to change what I am doing – because I don't want to change?

A. Before I answer this, please re-read Chapter 1 again very carefully. As a result of what is in store for most of us in the future, it is my sincere desire that no one becomes a victim of this looming crisis. My Mortgage Elimination™ System is so revolutionary that it will significantly improve your chances of NOT being caught in this predicament if you start NOW. However, it does require a little effort on your part because if you haven't made significant inroads in paying off your mortgage up until now, then the following adage may well apply to you - "if you keep doing what you've always done, then you'll always get what you've always gotten."

9. I'm a first-time homebuyer. How do I go about applying your Mortgage Elimination™ System?

A. The best thing would be to first find a P&I loan suitable for you, and then have the interest rate fixed, if that is what you choose. After that, you may want to apply the second option as a Mortgage Elimination™ strategy as referred to in Chapter 9 (Options For Consideration).

10. I already have a HELOC. Do I have to change to a new one?

A. No. As long as your HELOC complies with the characteristics I mentioned in Chapter 11 and my checklist (Chapter 12), you can use it with my Mortgage Elimination™ System, and you don't have to get a new one.

11. What do I have to do to get the Free 12 month subscription to use your online Mortgage Elimination™ Plan Software program?

A. First, you must apply for your HELOC directly through my website with one of the 'Affiliate Lenders' listed there. Next, your loan must be approved, settled, and we must receive your contact details and payment for the software usage fee from the lender with whom your loan was settled. As soon as we confirm this information with the lender, my team will e-mail you the login and password to access the online Mortgage Elimination™ Plan Software program, along with detailed instructions.

12. Can I still get the Free 12 month access to your software program if I already have a HELOC?

A. Unfortunately, no. The Free 12 month access is only available to people who apply for a **new HELOC directly through my website with one of the 'Affiliate Lenders' listed there**. Furthermore, your loan has to be approved, settled, and we must receive payment from the relevant lender for the 12 month subscription for use of the software program. However, you may want to use the $20, 30 day license to create your Mortgage Elimination™ Plan and then purchase additional licenses to update it as required. If you do this, and you want to update your plan after your 30 day license has expired, you won't have to reenter your entire details again because we will store your plan on our secure server for up to six months. All you have to do is reenter your login name and password and follow the prompts to renew your subscription.

13. **If I go through a mortgage broker to get my HELOC, can I still get the Free 12 months access to use your software program?**

A. Unfortunately, no. Please refer to the answer for questions 11 and 12.

14. **I already have a HELOC with one of the 'Affiliate Lenders' listed on your website. Can I still get the Free 12 months access to your software program?**

A. Unfortunately, no. Please refer to the answer for questions 11 and 12.

15. **I applied for my HELOC through your website with one of your 'Affiliate Lenders' listed there. My loan has been approved and settled. I have received my checkbooks and VISA Debit Cards, but I haven't received my login and password from you to access your online software program. What do I have to do to get these?**

A. Please go to my website and click on the 'Contact Us' link. Then select the appropriate form to send us your details. My team will verify this information with the appropriate lender and get back to you ASAP.

16. **I can't get a loan because I have a bad credit rating. What can I do?**

A. Quite simply, this question is really beyond the scope of this book because it has been covered in depth by many other authors. My best starting point for you would be to check out Suze Orman's excellent book, *The Courage To Be Rich,* as she discusses this topic in detail.

* * * * * * *

"The will must be stronger than the skill."

- Muhammad Ali -

Part D

Things to Consider

"The rung of a ladder was never meant to rest upon,
but only to support your weight long enough so
you can reach for something higher."

- Anonymous -

Phew!

I bet you're asking yourself, "What more can there be than what you've already told me, Harj?"

First, let me say that you have already learned the basic elements to make my Mortgage Elimination™ System work. However, if I were you and I really wanted to turbo-charge my journey to Own My Home Years Sooner, then I would definitely take the time to read the remaining information in this part of the book.

As I see it, if I can help you find one more dollar to put toward your mortgage, then that's one extra dollar that gets you closer to being free of that millstone around your neck. What's more, no $3,000 'consultant' is ever going to take the time to explain to you all of the additional things you can do to save extra interest on your home loan, and build wealth – as you are about to discover in this part of the book.

Second, I want you to get so much value for money from this book, that you won't be able to wait to tell all of your family and friends to get their own copy.

I know. I know.

I'm shameless in promoting my baby, and I make no apologies for it because I love what I do, and I love the fact that I may be able to help make a positive difference in someone's life. So, I hope you take an extra few minutes to read the remaining chapters, because even if you find just one idea that can save you more interest, it will help you Own Your Home Even Sooner.

"Continuous effort - not strength or intelligence is the key to unlocking our potential."

- Sir Winston Churchill -

Chapter 17
Saving Even More Interest

"Many people take no care of their money till they
come nearly to the end of it. And others
do just the same with their time."

- Goethe -

In this chapter, I will take you through some of the unique things my readers have done to really take advantage of our Key Principle to save even more interest, as well as to make money to put toward their HELOC.

Using the bank's money to save interest on your HELOC - at absolutely no cost to you!

Most people will tell you that the introduction of credit cards was the worst thing that ever happened to the western industrialized world. We have all heard horror stories of people owing large sums of money on credit cards and being charged exorbitant interest rates. However, it is my belief that credit cards per se are not at fault, but rather the way people use them, because when used wisely, they can actually save you money!

As you know, a lot of things can now be purchased on a 20 to 30-day interest free credit card. This means that you are not charged interest for the purchases until the interest free or 'grace' period is over.

Many people using my Mortgage Elimination™ System are also using credit cards for their budgeted expenses and paying for their purchases within the interest free period. This means that they are using the bank's money for their living expenses, while their money is left in their HELOC – which is reducing the principal – and therefore reducing the amount of interest they have to pay. Using credit cards also helps them to refine the accuracy of their Mortgage Elimination™ Plan because they get an itemized statement of their expenses each month that they can use to update their plans with.

A word of caution

If you have had trouble managing credit cards in the past, then DO NOT use them. The plan you created using my Mortgage Elimination™ Plan Software program deliberately does not include the use of credit cards. Using them to defer living expenses is just an added bonus.

However, if you have the self-discipline to handle credit cards and pay them off monthly, then you will be pleased to learn of other ingenious uses with which some of my readers have found.

Using 'smart money'

Once Bob and Nancy set up their HELOC and discovered how easily and quickly they could reduce the term of their home loan, they started to look for more ways to save interest. Besides using credit cards for their budgeted living expenses, here's what they came up with.

Bob is a golfing fanatic and plays a round every Saturday with his buddies. Collectively, they spend nearly $200 a week on golf. Bob collects cash from his golfing partners for their green fees and pays for the group with his credit card - which also earns him reward points!

At the first opportunity, he goes to the bank and deposits this money into his HELOC, which immediately reduces his principal and therefore reduces the amount of interest he has to pay.

In effect, Bob is using the bank's money to save interest on his HELOC and pays it back within the interest free period with absolutely no cost to him.

Bob and Nancy also do the same thing whenever they go out to dinner with their friends. They now carry very little cash with them and prefer to have their money working for them by leaving it in their HELOC.

Grocery shopping

Sherry has an elderly mother that she does the grocery shopping for every week. Her mother pays her cash for the groceries, and Sherry then charges them to her credit card. She deposits her mother's money into her HELOC straight away and pays for the groceries when she receives her credit card statement at the end of the month. She jokingly said she was thinking of doing the shopping for the entire retirement village this way.

If you don't have a relative you can do this for, then why not go shopping with your neighbor or friend and pay for their groceries on your credit card, and get them to give you the cash? If you're really brave, you can offer to do this for the person in front of you in line at the store.

HOT TIP

Difference between charge, debit, and credit cards

A 'Charge Card' carries no pre-set spending limit, and the statement balance must be paid in full at the end of the billing cycle (usually every month). The most recognized charge cards on the market today are American Express® and Diners Club®. A 'Debit Card' is like an ATM card that you have with your savings or checking account. With this type of card, you must have funds in the card account before you can make a withdrawal. In contrast, a 'Credit Card' carries a pre-set credit limit, and only a minimum (principal and interest) payment is required to be paid each month, and interest is applied to balances not cleared or paid in full.

Who are VISA® and MasterCard®?

These are the two major independent institutions that make the whole credit/debit card transaction system work.

Note that just because you have a VISA® or MasterCard® logo on your card does not mean that it's a 'Credit Card'. For example, you can have a VISA® Debit Card issued by your bank that allows you to take out cash from an ATM displaying the VISA® symbol and also to have it accepted by merchants like a regular credit card. This option gives you the best of both worlds - i.e., ability to take out cash and use it to buy goods. The only thing that you have to ensure is that the card account has sufficient funds in it at all times.

Who are MAESTRO® and CIRRUS®?

MAESTRO® is an international EFTPOS (Electronic Funds Transfer Point Of Sale) system. It let's you use your Maestro® Card to buy goods and services at any outlet displaying the Maestro® logo. You can also withdraw cash from an ATM displaying the Maestro® logo because it accesses the funds directly from your account.

CIRRUS® is an international ATM network. With your Cirrus® Card, you can withdraw cash and obtain account balances (in the local currency), at any ATM in the world displaying the Cirrus® logo.

Whenever using credit cards . . .

If you are thinking about using credit cards to defer payment for your living expenses, then here are the things you need to be aware of:

* A lot of people make the mistake of thinking that just because they have a credit card, they also automatically have an interest free period attached to it. This is not the case, so make sure that the credit card you have comes with an interest free or 'grace' period (usually around 20-30 days). Otherwise, you will be charged interest from the moment you make a purchase.

* Get a credit card with an interest free period that does not charge you a high account keeping fee ($0 - $30 per year is average).

* Never, ever use your credit card to withdraw cash. This is considered to be a "cash advance" (a loan), and the bank will start charging you interest at the maximum rate from the moment you make the transaction.

* Always pay the credit card bill as soon as you get your statement. Don't try to fiddle with the remaining interest free days to delay payment right up until the last moment. People have forgotten to pay, or they couldn't make it to the bank on the last day, and of course they are then hit with the interest. However, I have observed that most people only do this once.

Diamonds in your backyard

Another way that people have accelerated their Mortgage Elimination™ Plan is by selling unwanted household items and then injecting this money into their HELOC.

It's surprising how much you can make with those unnecessary items lying around your home. And before you think they have no value and take them to the dump, just remember the adage, "One man's trash is another man's treasure." You can offload these things through a simple garage sale, consignment store, or even through eBay, which is always a lot of fun. David and Sheryl (case study from Chapter 7) did this, made $954 and cut another 4 months off of their projected loan term – which also saved them another 4 months of interest.

So, how many diamonds can you find?

Discount offers

If you go to my website and click on 'Toolbox', you will find a whole host of everyday items and services that are available at a discounted price to 'turbo-charge' your Mortgage Elimination™ Plan (also see Appendix 4).

Imagine the effect on the term of your home loan if you can save even as little as $10 a month – every month – on a regular expense item. It may not sound like much, but it could cut years off your mortgage. What's more, my team is constantly finding and adding things to this webpage, so if you know of something that will save readers money, please drop me an e-mail.

Finally, if you have already signed up for my online newsletter, stay tuned to e-mail broadcasts from my team and me for updates on this exciting program.

How to get a loan for at least 3% below the variable home loan interest rate

You may have noticed that the interest you earn on your savings account is always a lot less than the interest you are charged on your home loan – because that's one of the ways the banks make their profits.

However, one of my clients, Steve, used this knowledge to his advantage to save a lot of money on his HELOC.

This is what he did.

His parents had nearly $19,000 in a cash management account earning 3.5% interest, and he had a large HELOC costing him 9.9%.

That worked out to be a difference of 6.4% in favor of the bank (i.e., 9.9% HELOC - 3.5% Cash Management Account = 6.4%).

Steve used my Mortgage Elimination™ Plan Software program to calculate that if he injected $19,000 into his HELOC and paid his parents the same interest they were earning with their cash management account, he would be the one coming out 6.4% in front.

That worked out to be a saving of over $100 in interest each month, which really meant $100 extra coming off of the principal of his loan each month.

Steve explained this to his parents and asked them if they planned to use their $19,000 in the near future. They said it was "for a rainy day" and liked the idea of having money available to them 'at call'.

Steve then explained to them that he had a Mortgage Elimination™ Plan, which doubled as his personal budget. He told them that if they put their money into his account, he would pay them the same interest as their current cash management account, and they would still have the money available to them 'at call' - albeit through his checkbook.

Steve's parents were only too glad to help out since there was really no difference to them in terms of the returns on their savings.

In effect, this method cost Steve 3.5% interest on $19,000 of his HELOC rather than 9.9% - not a bad interest rate for a loan, wouldn't you say? And even if he had paid his parents 4.5% interest, he would still have been 5.4% better off.

Having said all that, you can see that this case example is from the years when interest rates were higher than at the time of publication. Therefore, although the savings are not going to be as great during the periods when interest rates are low, it is a good ace to keep up your sleeve if interest rates take a turn for the worse – which they eventually will as part of the historical economic cycle.

A word of caution

Be aware that if you call any form of document a 'credit contract', or if you do something that makes the transaction have the appearance of you being in the business of lending money, that you could be violating certain regulations. So, please be careful in the way that you go about writing the repayment schedule to avoid this situation.

Furthermore, this method relies heavily on trust, and you don't want to lose friends and family members because of conflict over money. Therefore, if you are thinking of doing anything remotely like this, you may want to do the following to avoid any potential conflicts:

- Never try to force anyone to lend you the money. If you have explained how the concept works, they have read this book, and they still feel uncomfortable with the idea, then let them be. It's their money after all.

- No matter who it is, or how close you are to your 'lender', always, and I mean always, have something in writing. Make sure you outline the amount being borrowed and the terms and conditions of the 'loan'. Include how much interest you will pay the lender, when the interest will be paid, by what method it will be paid, and how the lender can have access to the money if and when they need it. Furthermore, it is a good idea to have a lawyer review this document to make sure it is sound. If you are a US or Canadian reader, please refer to Appendix 5 (Protect Yourself And Your Assets) for information on how you can do this for negligible cost to you.

- Finally, don't spend the interest savings. Stay within your projected monthly budget according to your Mortgage Elimination™ Plan, and leave the surplus in your HELOC. If your lender wants the money 'at call', you won't know when that call may come. But until it does, use the injected funds wisely because the interest you save will now be reducing the principal of your loan.

Sabotage proofing your HELOC

Some people may find that withdrawing money for their living expenses directly from their HELOC is too big of a transition from what they are used to. That is, they are unsure of whether they can keep their 'hand out of the cookie jar'.

One way to overcome this dilemma is to look at your budgeted expenses for each month from your Mortgage Elimination™ Plan and transfer that amount of money into a separate checking/savings account. Then only withdraw those living expenses from *that* account and no more.

You may ask, *"Doesn't that defeat the whole purpose of leaving all of my money in the home loan to reduce interest?"*

Yes, it does.

However, I have deliberately designed my online Mortgage Elimination™ Plan Software program to have certain built-in, conservative assumptions that are in your favor. That is, if you do what I have suggested (even though the best strategy is to leave your funds in your HELOC until you need them), you will still achieve your forecasted End of Month Loan Balances, as per your Mortgage Elimination™ Plan. If you're still skeptical, just try it out and see for yourself.

> *"If you think something small cannot make a difference,*
> *try going to sleep with a mosquito in the room."*
>
> *- Ben Hurn -*

Summary

It is said that necessity is the mother of all invention. And here are just some of the inventive ways my readers have come up with to save even more interest on their home loans. They have done this by taking further advantage of our Key Principle and generating extra income to pay off their loan quicker:

♦ Using credit cards to incur budgeted living expenses and deferring payment by utilizing the interest free or 'grace' period on the credit card. This means that their money sits in their HELOC for an extra 20-30 days, thereby reducing the principal for that period of time.

♦ Generating extra money to inject into their home loan through enterprises like garage sales.

♦ Asking relatives and friends to 'lend' them money, which is paid for at the same interest rate as the 'lender' would have earned through their savings account. Remember that the interest they earn in a savings account is a lot less than the interest you are charged on your home loan.

♦ Sabotage proofing their HELOC by only withdrawing their monthly budgeted living expenses as shown in their Mortgage Elimination™ Plan and not overspending.

"Creativity is the sudden cessation of stupidity."

- Dr. E. Land -

Chapter 18
The Wonder Loan

*"If you really want to do something, you will find a way.
If you don't, you will find an excuse."*

- Anon -

As you have rightly concluded, what I am endeavoring to convey here is that if you are willing to take charge of your personal financial lifestyle and change some of your old paradigms on how to pay back borrowed funds, then you can save a tremendous amount of time and money.

To that end, I consider a HELOC to be one of the greatest financial and wealth creation tools in existence today. So let me take a moment to share with you again just some of the many benefits of having this type of loan facility.

1. Income can be paid/transferred into your HELOC;
2. You can make interest only payments;
3. Tax deductibility;
4. Bargaining power;
5. It can save you money by being a lifelong facility.

1. Income can be paid/transferred into your HELOC

You can have your salary or regular income paid directly into your HELOC (if you have the right type), and you can access that money at call via a checkbook and ATM Debit Card. As I have mentioned, every cent that you leave in this type of account will reduce the principal of your loan, and therefore, reduce the amount of interest you will be charged. It will also have a compounding effect in reducing the term of your loan.

With standard P&I loans, this option is NOT available because once you make a repayment, your money is locked into the loan.

2. You can make interest only payments

With the right HELOC, your only obligation is to service the interest on the loan at the end of each month (i.e., monthly in arrears).

Remember, only the money used attracts interest - which is calculated on the daily balance. This is a great feature of this type of loan in that it gives you some degree of peace of mind in the event of unforeseen circumstances, such as losing your job. In this case, you have the option of only covering the interest payments until you can get back on your feet.

This is in contrast to P&I loans, which require you to make fixed principal and interest repayments on a periodic basis - without a great deal of flexibility.

3. Tax deductibility

As you know, interest on personal loans is NOT tax deductible. Examples of this include loans to purchase an automobile for personal use and credit card and installment interest incurred for personal expenses.

However, the IRS says, **borrowed funds that are secured by a taxpayer's primary or secondary residence**, such as second mortgages, HELOCs, and any other homeowner's debt, other than the first mortgage, are tax deductible.

Furthermore, the use of the home equity secured funds is not restricted, and you may use the money for any purpose, as long as the debt limits are not exceeded. As far as the current tax code is concerned, it allows a deductible limit of up to $100,000 for home equity debt ($50,000 for married individuals filing separate returns). Having said that, high-income earners do face some restrictions in deducting equity interest expense.

You can see that if you have high interest bearing personal loans or credit cards, or if you need to pay for your children's education, buy investments, or whatever, your home's equity can be a source of low interest, tax deductible funds to pay for these debts and expenses. However, rather than taking out a standard P&I loan to do all of this, you could use a HELOC and pay it off a lot sooner by using it in conjunction with the Mortgage Elimination™ Way.

For more information about the tax status of your home loans, go to the IRS website (www.irs.gov) and use their search engine by typing the words 'mortgage interest'. Lastly, make sure to consult with your accountant or financial advisor on this matter before taking action.

4. Bargaining power

We have all heard the adage, "money talks", but sometimes it downright shouts and screams.

Here's an example of what I mean.

Two of my readers who had been using my system for the past six years had built up a significant amount of equity in their home. They then decided to buy an investment property and found one that they liked. And because they had the money 'at call' through their HELOC, they made an offer to the seller for $35,000 less than the asking price for the property.

They said to the seller, "If you accept our price right now, we can have the check to you first thing tomorrow morning and close the deal."

The seller accepted the offer on the spot, and these people saved $35,000.

Just think, how long would it take for you to save that amount of money?

Furthermore, this is not only restricted to real estate deals. Many retailers will reduce the price of a product or service by up to 10%, sometimes more, if they know you can pay up front because they want to capture your business on the spot. This is the sort of bargaining power available to people who know how to use this type of loan product properly. You can also use this money saving strategy whenever a situation calls for a decision to be made, and the empowered position rests with the person who has control of both time and money – now, wouldn't you want that person to be you?

5. It can save you money by being a lifelong facility

Once you set up your HELOC, you can access your money up to the original limit at any time, for any purpose, at call. This also means that if you plan wisely, you can keep your HELOC as a lifelong facility to invest with.

As another example, let's say you decide to spend $10,000 to update your car in 5 years time.

In most cases, when people need money for this type of expense, they either save up for it, or take out a personal loan, which usually has an interest rate much higher than the prevailing interest rate for a HELOC. But with this type of loan, you can redraw the $10,000 by simply writing a check because your money's at call. The benefits of this option are rather obvious:

a) You will never have to go through the complicated process of loan approval ever again; and,

b) You will never have to pay for new loan setup costs ever again.

Summary

In conclusion, you can see that a HELOC - if used wisely - can be an extremely effective and efficient, long term, wealth creation tool.

Having said that, I also hope that you can see that this type of loan facility can only be effective if it is in the right hands! And as I have said numerous times now, make sure that if you are going to go ahead with implementing the Mortgage Elimination™ System as described in this book, that you are also willing to take total control of your financial affairs and have the right tools to do so properly. If you're willing to do that, then you better start thinking about what you're going to do with the extra income that will be freed up once you've Owned Your Home Years Sooner than you expected.

"Do, or do not ... there is no try."

- Master Yoda -

Chapter 19
International Readers

"Life is my college.
May I graduate well, and earn some honors!"

- Louisa May Alcott -

Steps 2 and 3 reversed

As I mentioned earlier, for you, I would recommend that Step 2 is 'Create Your Plan', and Step 3 is 'Get the Right Loan'. The reason for this is because at the time of publishing, we only had US lenders as part of our Lender Affiliate Program. These lenders have agreed to charge US residents a $0 application fee and closing costs for their HELOC, as well as pay for their software subscription fee. However, you may be charged hundreds of dollars in application fees for a HELOC in your country of residence. Therefore, before you spend any money on loan application fees, I recommend that you first create your plan to see if you like my system, and to determine how much money you will save. What's more, I have created an alternative, cost effective option so that you can do this. That is, rather than paying for a 6 or 12 month subscription fee for the software program, you can simply pay a one-time US$20 fee for a 30 day license that will allow you to create your Mortgage Elimination™ Plan (see details at end of chapter). Having said that, our Lender Affiliate Program is also open to non-US lenders who would like to be a part of it. If you are a lender who is interested in joining, please contact us by sending an email to the following address: Lenders@MortgageFreeUSA.com (please note the terms and conditions to join may be different for you).

Australian, New Zealand, and UK readers

In your respective countries you have an alternative loan product to the HELOC, which is just as effective in saving you interest - if you get one with the right features! It is called an *Interest Saver* or *Interest Offset Account.*

The way that these types of accounts work is instead of paying you interest on the balance in your savings account, the interest earned is used to reduce the interest charged on your P&I home loan. For example, let's assume you have a $100,000 home loan at 10% and $3,000 in one of these Interest Saver/Offset Accounts. In this case, the $3,000 in your Interest Saver/Offset Account will be 'offset' against $3,000 in your home loan, which will not be charged any interest at all (see diagram on next page).

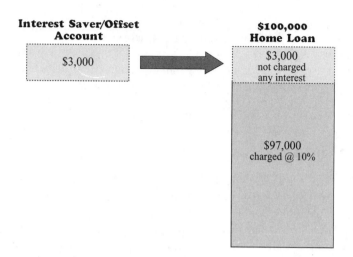

Interest Saver/Offset Account

$3,000

$100,000 Home Loan

$3,000
not charged
any interest

$97,000
charged @ 10%

Advantages of an Interest Saver/Offset Account

Even though I always say that a HELOC is an excellent, long term wealth creation tool, it does need to be managed wisely. If you feel that you may not have the discipline to handle such a loan facility, then you may want to consider an Interest Saver/Offset Account. That's because these types of loans still allow you to achieve exactly the same interest savings as a HELOC, as described in this book, and they also have the following advantages:

1. You are required to make regular repayments: The first thing to note about a P&I loan with a 'good' Interest Saver/Offset Account is that it is NOT a HELOC and therefore, it is NOT an interest-only loan. It is a P&I loan with set repayments, which you will regularly have to make at the end of each month (fortnight, or week);

2. You can only withdraw excess funds: Only the funds left in your Interest Saver/Offset Account are allowed to be withdrawn. Therefore, you are limited to how far you can dip into the pot, versus a HELOC where you can keep withdrawing funds right up to the original approved credit limit;

3. Makes full use of the Key Principle: These types of loans still allow you to take full advantage of our Key Principle because you can have all of your funds sitting in your Interest Saver/Offset Account until you need them. The 'good' ones even allow you to have your salary directly deposited into them, thereby saving you more interest on a daily basis.

HOT TIP

A major pitfall you have to watch out for is the terminology that some lenders use when they talk about their P&I loan having a '100% Offset Account.'

When I first heard about this, my initial reaction was, *"Great! That means that if I have $2 in my Interest Saver/Offset Account, then $2 of my home loan won't be charged any interest because that's a 100% offset - right?"*

Wrong!

Upon further examination, what this particular lender was actually saying was that if I had $2 in their Offset Account earning 3%, and the home loan was being charged 10%, then $2 of my home loan would be charged at 7% (i.e., 10% - 3% = 7%), because that was their idea of a '100% offset' on the 3% I would earn.

Sounds awfully confusing doesn't it?

You bet - but don't worry because all I'm trying to tell you here is that you can be duped in a few different ways into thinking that you have a particular loan product when you actually don't. So, if you are looking for this type of loan, make sure that you take with you my checklist (at the end of this chapter) of what to look for in a 'good' Interest Saver/Offset Account, and make sure that you get a tick in every box. Otherwise, you may find yourself with an ineffective loan.

Blessing for UK readers

In your country, you have perhaps one of the best home loan products that I have ever come across in all of my years in this industry. It is an excellent variation of the Interest Saver/Offset Account and is called *Offset Together*.

In effect, what this particular loan product allows you to do is have up to 11 family and friends link their savings/offset accounts to your mortgage. The balances in their accounts are then offset against the balance of your home loan. For example, let's say you have a £100,000 home loan and find 11 family and friends with £2,000 each. The collective monies in their offset accounts adds up to £22,000. When this is offset against your mortgage, you only pay interest on £78,000 (see diagram below).

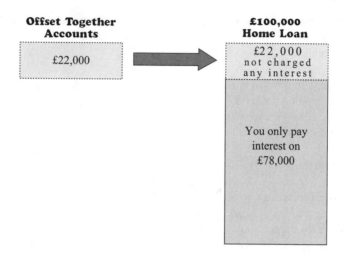

Offset Together Accounts	£100,000 Home Loan
£22,000	£22,000 not charged any interest
	You only pay interest on £78,000

If I was a UK resident, I would give this loan product some very serious consideration and then set about finding family and friends who would be willing to help me Own My Home Years Sooner.

For updates about whether lenders in your country of residence have joined our affiliate program, please go to my website, click on 'What to do', and from the drop down menu select 'Step 2 - Get the Right Loan'. Once on this page, click on 'Review Affiliate Lenders' for more information.

Note to Australian & New Zealand readers

In addition to the Interest Saver/Offset Account, you have another type of loan product available to you in your countries called a *Redraw Account.*

These accounts work a bit differently to the Interest Saver/Offset Account I just described. That is, they simply allow you to pay extra money toward the principal of your home loan - *above your standard repayment* - and then withdraw that money if and when you need it - without having to refinance your entire loan.

The advantages of Redraw Accounts

- Placing your funds in a Redraw Account is a very effective method of reducing the daily balance of your home loan and therefore, reducing the amount of interest you have to pay.

- It will result in returns equivalent to the interest rate of your home loan.

- Because you will be saving interest as opposed to earning interest, you will not have to pay tax on the interest saved.

The many disadvantages of Redraw Accounts

- Most lenders insist that you have a minimum of $2,000 in a Redraw Account before that money is offset against your home loan;

- If the balance in your Redraw Account falls below $2,000 at any time then you no longer qualify for the offset benefits. Worse still, you don't earn any interest on the rest of the money in the account either;

- Most institutions will not allow you to have a Redraw Account while you are in a fixed interest rate or 'honeymoon' period of your loan;

- With regards to withdrawals, most lenders have one of two policies:

    (a) You either have to pay a fee to access your money (between $10 - $50 per withdrawal); or,

    (b) You have to withdraw a minimum amount each time (between $500 - $2,000 per withdrawal).

- Finally, watch out for hefty monthly or yearly account keeping fees with many lenders.

Although having a Redraw Account attached to your P&I Loan is better than having nothing at all, there are usually a lot of disadvantages associated with this type of loan facility. Therefore, you might want to settle for an Interest Saver/Offset Account - with the features as described on my checklist at the end of this chapter.

"The degree of one's emotion varies inversely with one's knowledge of the facts - the less you know the hotter you get."

- Bertrand Russell -

Checklist for a 'Good' Interest Saver/Offset Account

In order to prevent yourself from signing up for an 'inferior' Interest Saver/Offset Account, make sure you take this checklist with you to ensure that the loan you are being offered has all of the features listed below. If not, then shop around until you find one that does. You may also want to visit my website for updates on whether lenders in your country have joined our 'Lender Affiliate Program'. To do this simply go to my website, click on 'What to do', and from the drop down menu click on 'Step 2 - Get the Right Loan'. Once on this page, click on 'Review Affiliate Lenders' for more information.

❑ The interest earned on the Interest Saver/Offset Account is the *same* as the interest charged on your home loan. Another way to phrase this is, *"if you have $10 in your Interest Saver/Offset Account, then $10 of your home loan will not be charged any interest at all."*

❑ Some lenders require you to have a minimum amount ($500 - $3,000) in your Interest Saver/Offset Account before the interest is offset against your home loan. Therefore, you need to make sure that there is no minimum amount necessary in the Interest Saver/Offset Account being offered before your lender will offset the interest on your home loan.

❑ There are no restrictions on how much or how many times you can deposit or withdraw each time from your Interest Saver/Offset Account, and there are no 'per transaction' fees to do so.

❑ Your lender will allow you to have an Interest Saver/Offset Account while you are in the 'honeymoon' or discounted interest rate period.

❑ You can have your salary or wages paid directly into this type of account, thereby offsetting more of your home loan and saving you money because it is not being charged any interest.

❑ There are minimal ($8 per month) or no account keeping fees at all.

Summary

At the time of publishing this edition, we were in the process of 'courting' non-US lenders to be a part of our 'Lender Affiliate Program', so that you, our international readers, could also receive similar benefits as your US counter-parts. If you want to find out which lender(s) from your country have joined our Affiliate Program, and the sorts of benefits they are offering, simply go to my website, click on 'What to do', and from the drop down menu click on 'Step 2 - Get the Right Loan'. Once on this page, click on 'Review Affiliate Lenders' for more information.

Meanwhile, if you find that none of the lenders from your country of residence have joined our program yet, you may want to exercise the option I suggested in terms of reversing Steps 2 and 3. That is, create your Mortgage Elimination™ Plan before you apply for a loan and spend hundreds of dollars on loan application fees. To do this, simply go to my website, click on 'What to do', and from the drop down menu select 'Step 3 - Create Your Plan'. Once on this page, click on 'Subscribe Now', and then simply select the option for the $20, 30 day licence.

Furthermore, if you are a reader from Australia, New Zealand, or the UK, lenders from your countries have already expressed interest in becoming our affiliate partners, and it is only a matter of time before you will be enjoying benefits from them. If you decide to apply for an Interest Saver/Offset Account before we have signed up any lenders, make sure you use my check-list to find a suitable loan product.

*"The happiest people don't necessarily have
the best of everything. They just make
the best of everything."*

- Anonymous -

*"Twenty years from now you will be
more disappointed by the things you didn't do
than by the ones you did.
So throw off the bowlines.
Sail away from the safe harbor.
Catch the trade winds in your sails.
Explore. Dream."*

- Mark Twain -

The Final Word

*"All the time, Destiny is within one's grasp.
Through action. Determined, committed action."*

- *William James Scully* -

We began this journey talking about making dreams come true.

Just take a moment again to imagine having the freedom to do all of the things you want to do when your home loan is no longer an obstacle in your life.

That would be wild, wouldn't it?

Or, alternatively, think about saving enough interest that it is equivalent to a full year's salary. Imagine what you could do with all that money.

Now, I know from personal experience that you may be feeling somewhat reluctant right now. You may be saying to yourself, "Am I really going to save that much money?", or, "That would be nice, but it all seems a bit too hard."

In response to that, all I can say to you is what I used to say to all of my clients in my consulting days, and that is, numbers don't lie. What's more, neither of us will know how much time and interest you will save unless you follow through with all three steps and create your Mortgage Elimination™ Plan.

Having said that, I also understand that changing the way you think about paying off your home loan is a very personal matter. You had to do a lot of running around to get the loan in the first place. It took time to read and sign all those documents, and finally, everything's going well. And the last thing you want to do is to think about it again.

Furthermore, you may have even discussed some of this information with family and friends and received negative feedback. I guarantee you the first thing most of them will say is, *"Oh yeah, I know all about that. It's one of those bi-weekly repayment plans."*

Whenever you get this response – which will be often - don't try to get into a debate with the person. Just be aware that you now know at this stage a lot more than most people in this country about how to eliminate your mortgage, including most of the lenders.

Furthermore, if the person persists in pushing their point of view, just ask yourself this one simple question: are they saving tens of thousands of dollars in interest on their home loan?

Let me give you an anecdote from my own recent experience.

I have a relative who is one of the most intelligent, willful, persuasive, charming, and powerful people I have ever known. These qualities may also explain why he is the best operator in his chosen occupational field in his country of residence.

This person has known for the last seven years that I am a best selling author on mortgage reduction strategies in the country, and has also known how many people have been helped through my publications. However, his lethargy has kept him from ever asking me to look at his financial situation.

To cut a long story short, early last year, I went back to Australia for my youngest brother's engagement. One morning at breakfast, my mother in her exuberance, told this relative about my latest appearance on a national current affairs program who did another story about my Mortgage Elimination™ System. We started making small talk, and he finally came out and asked me how to structure his loans.

It turned out that in addition to his residential property, he had three investment properties, five different loans, including a business loan, and thousands of dollars in cash in the bank – doing nothing. It took about five minutes for me to see where he could save money by restructuring his finances and using my system. However, it took almost two hours for me to explain this to him because he kept interrupting me with what he thought should happen.

Well, do you know how much money he had been losing in the form of interest each year because of his lethargy?

We calculated it to be $15,000 a year.

Worst of all, he had been doing this for the last five years, which meant $15,000 x 5 years = $75,000 lost in interest that never had to be paid – ever!

Ouch!

So my recommendation to you is . . .

Let others be insane

By the way, do you know what insanity is?

Insanity is all about doing the same thing, day in and day out, and expecting different results.

So how many people do you know who are doing the same thing with their home loan and expecting to pay them off sooner?

But you know, forget about other people because the most important person here is you. And the question you should really be asking is, "Am I doing the same thing with my home loan and expecting different results?"

Talking about detractors . . .

Don't expect support from your local lenders either

I don't mean to engage in bank-bashing here, but this is a fact.

The reason is because my Mortgage Elimination™ System is so new in most countries that a lot of lenders will not have heard about it - yet.

Remember Mrs. C.E. Tranent from Chapter 10?

She's the only person ever to ask for her money back after buying my book. That's because when she went to her bank and tried to get a HELOC by explaining my system, the bank staff told her, *"they will not be a party to any such scheme."* And five years later, the bank in question developed a loan product in accordance with my criteria for a 'good' HELOC and used similar verbiage from this book to promote it.

So if you go to the branch of your local lender and try to explain what you're attempting to do, don't be surprised if you are met with a lot of blank expressions and silly replies to your informed questions. By the way, here are two of the most common responses you can expect.

"You can achieve the same results with a P&I loan."

Some lenders and financial writers will tell you that you can achieve the same results I have outlined by using a standard P&I loan. Technically, this is possible. However practically, it is virtually impossible. The reason is that you would have to inject every cent you earn into your P&I loan. This means that your money will be locked into the loan, and you will not be able to access it other than by way of refinancing. Alternatively, with a HELOC, you will not only gain the interest savings, but you can also access your funds for living expenses – at call.

"These types of loans are not safe because you have to budget."

Once you create your Mortgage Elimination™ Plan, you will be able to see exactly how much time and money you could save. For most people, this is enough of an incentive to stick to their plan and fulfill it. Furthermore, I have found that by having a Mortgage Elimination™ Plan and using my software program, people become much more conscious of their finances and achieve their forecasted results. That's because they start making much more informed decisions about how to spend their money by using this tool.

You know, you can avoid a lot of frustration by not blaming the lenders because they don't know what you now know. As I said, it will take them about four years to catch up and acknowledge that this system has merit. Then watch out for the plethora of ads on TV and radio, and in magazines and newspapers with the heading "Own Your Home Years Sooner – we'll show you how."

In the meanwhile, save yourself a lot of time and effort by using the 'Affiliate Lenders' listed on my website because they know what you are trying to achieve and have the loan products to support it.

So let us leave the harbingers of skepticism behind with this most apt quote:

> *"The cynic is his own worst enemy. It requires far less skill to run a wrecking company than it does to be an architect."*
>
> *- U.S. Andersen -*

Let your life be your prayer

This is the advice a very wise friend once gave me, and I endeavor to live by it every day. He also said to me, *"Harj, if you want to be successful, hang around with successful people."* Have you noticed that this is actually true? So in turn, my advice to you is - don't listen to negative chatter, including the stuff in your head, and don't hang around with anyone who says you can't do this.

That brings me to my next point. I've found that there is safety in numbers.

Let me explain.

I visited an old friend at his workplace recently, and he introduced me to a few of his colleagues. He said that once he had set up his Mortgage Elimination™ Plan and saw how much money he would save, he started telling everyone else in the office about it. Pretty soon they were all talking about my system and collectively helped each other to follow through with it. And now, they're all doing great.

If you find yourself in a similar position, then by all means I encourage you to start your own little revolution. My friend said that the best thing he could share with others was what he was doing successfully in his own life. He said, *"My monthly loan statements are living proof that my plan is working for me."* He is also on his way to owning his second investment property. Tell me, how can you argue against that? By the way, I forgot to mention one of the most important points and that is . . .

What have you got to lose?

I've designed my system so that it's easy to understand and apply. And if you do everything correctly, the only out of pocket expense you should incur is the price of this book. If you use one of the 'Affiliate Lenders' through my website to apply for your loan, you will pay $0 for your HELOC application fee (in most cases). Furthermore, your entire first year's subscription to the Mortgage Elimination™ Plan Software program will be paid for if your loan settles with one of the 'Affiliate Lenders' listed on my website (see Chapters 13 and 14 for details). This will save you an additional $200 in the first year, and at the time of publishing, I was negotiating with lenders to have this fee paid on your behalf for the duration of your HELOC - saving you an additional $200 every year thereafter! Now how can you argue against that when you could have wasted $3,000 on a consultant?

Inspiration and updates

Finally, to help keep you inspired, my team and I will send you email newsletters and success stories of readers who are Owning Their Homes Years Sooner. That way, you can see how others are doing, and you can pick up more tips on accelerating your own Mortgage Elimination™ Plan. I would also encourage you to regularly use the Mortgage Elimination™ Plan Software program on my website to make informed decisions about your money, and still enjoy your life. For example, one couple shared the following story with me.

Maria and Brent were a bit concerned that they would have to keep a tight reign on their finances in order to make their plan work. They had two children – one aged five, the other seven – and they wanted to take the kids to Disneyland while they were young enough to enjoy it.

This adventure was going to cost the family around $10,000.

However, they didn't want to wait another six years until they had paid off their home loan before going on this family adventure. Instead, they wanted to go within the first two years of starting their Mortgage Elimination™ Plan.

So, they factored the trip as a Lump Sum Expense in the online software program, and it showed that spending this amount of money would increase their loan term by another eleven months.

They decided the holiday would definitely be worth the extra time because of the joy it would bring them as a family ... so they went!

The point I want to make is that I don't want you to miss out on the finer things in life either. I just want you to be able to make informed decisions so you don't have to work all of your life for your mortgage. Use my tools. Make your money work harder for you instead. This is such a worthy thing that you can do for yourself and your family, and every day you put it off is another day that money is going out of your pocket on unnecessary interest payments. With all of these resources available to you, you too can join the tens of thousands of people who are Owning Their Homes Years Sooner - without making extra interest payments. The only question is, do you want to?

Before you go . . .

I have a small favor to ask of you - and I hope you can help me out.

You see, a lot of people say to me; *"How come you virtually give this information away when there are consultants out there charging $3,000+ for this type of program?"* Well, the reason my team and I can get this information out to you is because we don't spend huge amounts of money on marketing or advertising. Instead, we rely on you, our customers, to tell your family and friends about us and this book.

So, will you tell 3-6 friends about your experience with this book?

Now, I cannot know, of course, whether or not you follow through. But if you do, you will not only help me out, but also help to revolutionize the entire lending industry in this country to bring about better loan products that will benefit everyone. In return, my team and I promise to keep you updated with the latest Insider Secrets and knowledge that you have been exposed to in this book and on my website. You know, a really easy way you can help spread the word is by simply downloading sample chapters of this book from my website, and sending them to people on your e-mail list. I can personally GUARANTEE you that they'll be glad you did.

In conclusion

My team and I are very much looking forward to welcoming you to my website as members. We wish you and your loved ones the very best in Owning Your Homes Years Sooner and saving thousands of dollars in interest as well. And, as you make your way through this wonderful adventure called Life, always remember . . .

> *"Believe nothing.*
> *No matter who said it, Not even if I have said it.*
> *Unless it agrees with your own reason*
> *and your own understanding."*
>
> *- Guatama -*

Harj Gill
CEO - American Mortgage Eliminators™, LLC

p.s. If you would like to share with me your story of how well this system is working for you, I would love to hear from you. Simply send me an e-mail to the following e-mail address - Success@MortgageFreeUSA.com. Also, I would really appreciate it if you would be so kind as to leave a review of this book on the Amazon.com website.

HSBC Bank ad, *The West Australian* (March 25, 2003)

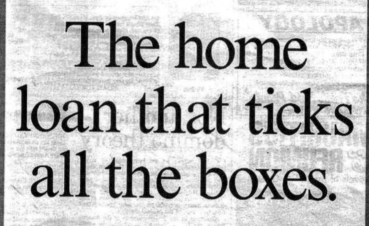

The home loan that ticks all the boxes.

☑ Competitive rate.
☑ No ongoing fees.
☑ All-in-one account.
☑ Instant access to funds.
☑ Payment flexibility.

We think HSBC's Home Smart Home Loan has everything. Money Magazine seems to agree, awarding our Home Smart Home Loan 'Best all-in-one Home Loan' in their 'Best of the Best for 2003' Awards.

Maybe it's because, as one of the world's largest providers of home loans in over 80 countries, we understand what you're looking for from your home loan.

Only 5.58%' p.a. interest for the first 12 months, no ongoing fees, instant funds access and payment flexibility all in one account.

And every enquiry before May 9th 2003 will receive a free copy of Harj Gill's book 'How to be mortgage free in 4 easy steps.'

Simply call **1300 131 603**, visit our website **www.hsbc.com.au/freebook** or pop into your nearest branch.

See enlargement
of text
on next page

HSBC ⟨X⟩
The world's local bank

Enlargement from previous page

We think HSBC's Home Smart Home Loan has everything. Money Magazine seems to agree, awarding our Home Smart Home Loan 'Best all-in-one Home Loan' in their 'Best of the Best for 2003' Awards.

Maybe it's because, as one of the world's largest providers of home loans in over 80 countries, we understand what you're looking for from your home loan.

Only 5.58%* p.a. interest for the first 12 months, no ongoing fees, instant funds access and payment flexibility all in one account.

And every enquiry before May 9th 2003 will receive a free copy of Harj Gill's book 'How to be mortgage free in 4 easy steps.'

Simply call 1300 131 603, visit our website www.hsbc.com.au/freebook or pop into your nearest branch.

Only 5.58%* p.a. interest for the first 12 months, no ongoing fees, instant funds access and payment flexibility all in one account.

And every enquiry before May 9th 2003 will receive a free copy of Harj Gill's book 'How to be mortgage free in 4 easy steps.'

Simply call 1300 131 603, visit our website www.hsbc.com.au/freebook or pop into your nearest branch.

Appendix 2
Affiliate Program - Lenders

Open invitation

Our Lender Affiliate Program is open to any lender in the world*.

For US lenders, here are the general criteria you need to satisfy in order to become our affiliate partner:

1. Have a Home Equity Line of Credit (HELOC) with as many of the features mentioned in this book, so that it is suitable for use with our Mortgage Elimination™ System. Please refer to Chapter 11 and the checklist for a 'Good' HELOC on page 92 for more information. You may also want to visit our website to view how these HELOC features are displayed. To do this, simply go to our website, click on the menu item 'What to do', select 'Step 2 – Get the right loan', and then select 'Review Affiliate Lenders'.

2. Charge our readers a $0 application fee and $0 closing costs for your HELOC.

3. Pay the yearly subscription fee on behalf of applicants to access our online Mortgage Elimination™ Plan Software program – upon successful settlement of their HELOC - preferably for the duration of their HELOC term.

4. Have your HELOC application page linked directly from the 'Affiliate Lender' page on our website.

5. Allocate a specific person and help-line to deal directly with our readers/customers who may need assistance with any aspect of their HELOC application.

If the above terms and conditions are acceptable to you and you wish to be accepted as an affiliate lending partner, please contact us through the following e-mail address: Lenders@MortgageFreeUSA.com, and someone will assist you in completing the affiliate process, and/or answer any further questions you may have.

We look forward to welcoming you on board.

* Different criteria apply for non-US lenders. Please contact us for further information.

Appendix 3
Affiliate Program - Partners

Earn easy money

According to the 2000 US Census, there are more than 38 million mortgaged households in the United States. Just ask yourself this question: *do you think every one of these people would like to Own Their Homes Years Sooner?*

You bet – and you can help them do just that – and get paid for it!

How?

By joining our 'Partner Affiliate Program'.

When you become our affiliate partner, you will not only generate extra income for yourself and enhance the value of your website, you will also be telling your visitors about a great product that can help them achieve their dream of accelerated home ownership.

By referring your visitors to our website, **www.MortgageFreeUSA.com**, you will earn a commission whenever they click-through from your website and purchase a copy of our best selling book, *"How to Own Your Home Years Sooner – without making extra interest payments."* When visitors from your website do this, our Partner Affiliate Program will pay you up to 20% for every sale, making it one of the most rewarding affiliate programs on the Internet today*. The best part is that our affiliate program is **FREE to join!**

In order to ensure that you are rewarded for your efforts in a timely manner, our affiliate program is conducted and monitored by Commission Junction, a highly reputable third party that is an industry leader in pay-for-performance marketing. And all you need to become an affiliate is to have a live website and a little HTML knowledge.

Now what could be easier than that? So join today – and start earning easy money!

All you have to do now is log on to our website, click on the menu item 'Affiliates', select 'Partner program', and then follow the simple step-by-step directions to join.

---

* Publisher's note: although our book refers to the banking and mortgage industries in the United States, the practical application of the Mortgage Elimination™ System can be utilized in any country.

Appendix 4
Toolbox · Save More Money

When you visit our website, you will see a navigation item along the top bar that says 'Toolbox'.

When you click on this link, you will see a range of products and services that we believe will help make your life easier and/or save you money - which you can then put toward your home loan - so you can pay it off even sooner.

What's more, we are continually adding to this list of products and services. So if you know of something that will save money for readers like you, we'd like to hear about it. If you are a vendor who has something to offer our readers and visitors that will save them money, then we would like to hear from you too.

For suggestions, comments, and more information (for potential vendors), please send an e-mail to Toolbox@MortgageFreeUSA.com.

We look forward to hearing from you.

Appendix 5
Protect Yourself and Your Assets

If you complete the three steps of our Mortgage Elimination™ System, you know that your asset base is going to grow a lot faster than what you had originally thought possible. Therefore, we strongly recommend that you take the necessary precautions to build a legal firewall around what you have worked so diligently to create for you and your family.

The reason we are going into detail on this topic is because, sadly, we have seen too many people get taken advantage of much too often, both financially and emotionally, because they didn't know their legal rights - nor did they have access to legal counsel - at call. Have a look at the set of everyday situations below. We guarantee that during the course of a year, you will encounter at least one of them.

✓ You will sign at least one legal contract;
✓ You may receive an inaccurate credit rating or report;
✓ You may be asked to pay a bill that you know is unfair;
✓ You may purchase a faulty product or service, and the company refuses to honor the warranty;
✓ You may be asked to pay a repair bill that is not the amount you originally authorized;
✓ You may be charged with a traffic violation;
✓ You may want to make a legal Will;
✓ If you already have a legal Will, you may want to update it;
✓ You may have a problem with an insurance claim.

Now even if you encounter only one of these situations, you know that the ramifications can be potentially devastating if something goes wrong. You could not only end up losing your home, but your livelihood as well, as you take your battle through the legal system, that could potentially cost you and your family thousands of dollars to resolve – even if you're not at fault!

You've heard the adage, "An ounce of prevention is worth a pound of cure?" Well if you live in the United States or Canada, there is a way you can protect your legal rights for less than the price of a cup of coffee a day. Here is a brief description of the services one company offers it's members. . .

Peace of mind at an affordable price

The following is what one company offers its members for around $17 per month:

✓ Unlimited phone consultations whenever you want to talk to an attorney who specializes in the area you have questions about. You can call once a month, once a week, or as many times a day as needed.

✓ If the situation demands it, an attorney will write a letter or make a phone call on your behalf – and will do this for you on an unlimited number of personal legal issues.

✓ If there is anything you ever have to sign, an attorney will review an unlimited number of these documents, up to 10 pages in length. You can ask him/her to counsel you on three things: What does it mean? Is it in your best interest to sign it? If not, what needs to be changed?

✓ Whenever you are out of State on business or pleasure and you need to speak with an attorney on any legal issue, you simply dial an 800 number. You are then put into contact with a local attorney who is qualified to counsel you in accordance with the laws of the State you happen to be in at the time.

✓ An attorney also helps you to complete a legal Will and reviews and updates it, if necessary, on an annual basis.

✓ If you happen to be involved in a moving traffic violation of any nature, in any State, you can call an attorney for assistance.

✓ In the event that someone files a civil lawsuit against you, you have access of up to 60 hours of a lawyer's time. What's more, the number of hours you are allocated increases each year for up to a total of 300 hours in the 5th year of your membership*.

✓ You have up to 50 hours of a lawyer's time if you receive notice of an IRS audit*.

✓ Heaven forbid, but in the unfortunate event that you or your spouse ever get arrested or taken into custody (although certain conditions apply here), you can call a toll-free number and have 24-hour access to an attorney for assistance. This coverage is also available to you on a nationwide level.

* This is not available in every State. Refer to your State of residence for full details.

There are more benefits this company offers such as Identity Theft Protection. However, we are not going to go into full details about them because we want to give you some background information about the company.

Background: Pre-Paid Legal Services®, Inc.

In order to investigate in depth, the company in question and the quality of the services it provides, the author of this book became a subscribing member of the company's services. Here is what he found . . .

Pre-Paid Legal Services®, Inc. was formed in 1972 by Harland C. Stonecipher and is based in Ada, Oklahoma.

Basically, this company offers a pre-paid plan much like what you would pay for your health insurance coverage. However in this case, it is for legal services, which this company has pioneered in introducing as a concept to ordinary Americans since it was founded.

In 1979, the company filed with the Securities and Exchange Commission (SEC) to register its securities for sale to the public, and its stock became available over the counter on the NASDAQ Exchange. In October 1986, the company's stock moved to the American Exchange (AMEX), and on May 13, 1999, the company began listing its stock on the New York Stock Exchange (NYSE).

The company is solid and continues to grow financially. Furthermore, it has received rave reviews from major independent publications such as *Fortune, Forbes, Money,* and *Success* magazines, which have all applauded its fiscal performance since being listed as a public company.

Cost and number of users

Quite simply, if you want to use the service, you pay a monthly membership fee of around $16*, which entitles you to all of the benefits mentioned earlier and more. However, not all States charge the same fee, and some of the legal services offered may vary slightly from State to State – although the differences are not dramatic.

As of July 22, 2003:

- The company had over 1.2 million subscribing members spread throughout the United States, excluding Alaska. It also offers this service in the Canadian provinces of Alberta, British Columbia, Manitoba, and Ontario.

- Collectively, there were 27,308 State and Corporate bodies that were offering the Pre-Paid Legal Service® membership as a group benefit to their employees, including some of the largest public companies in the United States.

- Every State government, except Alaska and New Hampshire, is offering the Pre-Paid Legal Service® as a group benefit to their employees.

* This is the price for a 'Standard Family Plan'. For an extra $1 per month, you can apply for the 'Legal Shield Rider', which gives you 24-hour access to an attorney in case you are arrested or taken into custody (conditions apply). There are also other plans available for different States that vary in price and the benefits you are entitled to.

The service and quality control

Quite logically, you should ask yourself, *"what kind of lawyer can you really get for $17 dollars a month, and what is the quality of the law firms that are associated with this company?"*

In answer to these questions, we found that the company screens and selects a quality law firm in each State (although some States have a different arrangement) and pays them a hefty retainer. Each firm is also given the mandate that they should treat every Pre-Paid Legal Services® member with the same level of respect and service as if the member was a major client. Furthermore, in order to ensure quality service and control, the law firm's contract is reviewed and renewed every 45 days. If they don't perform, their contract is terminated. However, turnover of law firms is extremely low.

How can you become a member?

If you, your family, or your friends wish to sign up for a Pre-Paid Legal Services® membership, you can do so directly through our website.

Here are the instructions to becoming a member:

1. Go to our website at www.MortgageFreeUSA.com, click on 'What to do', and select 'Join Pre-Paid Legal Services®, Inc.'

2. Once the page loads, read the instructions, and click on 'Become Member'.

3. You will then be directed to a Pre-Paid Legal Services®, Inc., Independent Associate webpage where you will be guided through the membership subscription process. Here you can 'View the Movie', which tells you more about Pre-Paid Legal Services®, Inc., and you can also 'Enroll' for the service online.

4. Once you click on 'Enroll' online, a new page will load on your screen that asks you to select the State or Province in which you reside. Once

you have done this, click on 'Go', and you will see the different plans available for your State or Province.

5. Under the 'Featured Plans' you will see an "Expanded Family Plan" ($25/month + one-time $10 enrollment fee) and a "Standard Family Plan" ($16/month + one-time $10 enrollment fee). Please note that not all States offer the Expanded Family Plan at this time, and the only difference between the Standard and Expanded Family Plans is that you receive more pre-trial and trial defense hours with the Expanded Family Plan. Also, the cost of the plan differs for Canadian Provinces. To review the full service available for each plan, simply click on the underlined options, and a pop-up screen will outline the benefits of the plan selected.

6. When you have decided on the plan that is most suitable for your needs, simply follow through with the remaining steps of the enrollment process.

> *"It is useless for sheep to pass a resolution*
> *in favor of vegetarianism*
> *when wolves remain of a different opinion."*
>
> *- William Randolph Inge -*

PUBLISHER'S NOTE: Due to the independent nature of the research carried out by the author on Pre-Paid Legal Services®, Inc., the company asked that the following disclaimer be included in this book:

1) Pre-Paid Legal Services®, Inc. does not endorse MortgageFreeUSA.com

2) This book's author is an Independent Associate of Pre-Paid Legal Services®, Inc. Pre-Paid Legal Services®, Inc. has not reviewed the comments within this chapter for accuracy. Readers are encouraged to obtain a membership contract from the applicable State for a complete review of the benefits provided, as well as exclusions.

Appendix 6
Nature of Relationship with Affiliate Lenders

♦ The nature of the relationship between American Mortgage Eliminators™, LLC and the Affiliate Lending Partners listed on its website will be solely to provide access for customers to American Mortgage Eliminators™, LLC online software program – upon payment of the subscription fee by an Affiliate Lending Partner on behalf of customers.

♦ American Mortgage Eliminators™, LLC is NOT a mortgage broking firm and will not offer individual advice nor consult about the appropriateness of the loans offered by the Affiliate Lenders listed on its website.

♦ American Mortgage Eliminators™, LLC is a COMPLETELY INDE-PENDENT company and is NOT an employee, agent, or representative of any of the Affiliate Lenders listed on its website, nor is it engaged in a joint venture with them.

♦ ALL loan application procedures and processes are solely between the Lender and the Applicant and the sole responsibility of the parties concerned.

♦ ALL inquiries relating to any loans applied though American Mortgage Eliminators™, LLC website is the sole responsibility of the relevant Affiliate Lender and should be directed to the customer support department of that Affiliate Lender.

♦ Any inquiries relating to the use of the online Mortgage Elimination™ Plan Software program is the sole responsibility of American Mortgage Eliminators™ , LLC and should be directed to "Tech support" as listed in the Member's Area of the company's website.

About the Author
Harj Gill (M.Ed)

Harj Gill enrolled at the University of Western Australia in 1983 where he graduated with a Masters Degree in the field of Organizational Planning and Change.

He started in the mortgage reduction industry as a consultant before specializing in the field and becoming a director of his own company.

His vision was to reach out to as many people as possible with his insider knowledge of the banking and mortgage industries, so that the power of home ownership would be in the hands of individuals.

In February 1997, his first book, titled, *"How to Own Your Home Years Sooner - without making extra payments",* was launched and instantly became a Best Seller.

Over the past six years, he has turned his original vision into Australia's largest, integrated online and publishing organization that is completely dedicated to helping people Own Their Homes Years Sooner.

American Mortgage Eliminators™, is the company he set up to introduce his revolutionary Mortgage Elimination™ System to the Global audience.

How to Order

US Customers:

This book has just been introduced to the US and is most likely NOT in your local bookstore - yet. Therefore, we suggest that you may want to order directly through our website. As an added incentive for doing this, we usually have great offers for our online customers. To make a purchase and find out about the latest offers, visit us at www.MortgageFreeUSA.com.

International Customers:

Once again, this book is most likely NOT in your local bookstore, and if you would like a copy, we suggest the following:

1. Go to our website www.MortgageFreeUSA.com

2. Click on "Buy Now".

3. Then click on "INTERNATIONAL VISITORS click here to order" (at the top of the online order form).

Bulk Orders:

This book is also available at quantity discounts. If you would like further information, please send an e-mail to Orders@MortgageFreeUSA.com